Nightmares and Visions

··◦❦Nightmares and Visions❦◦··

Flannery O'Connor
and the Catholic Grotesque

Gilbert H. Muller

University of Georgia Press

Athens

Library of Congress Catalog Card Number: 75-184777
International Standard Book Number: 0-8203-0284-8

The University of Georgia Press, Athens 30601

Printed in the United States of America
by The TJM Corporation
Baton Rouge, Louisiana 70806

Excerpts from the work of Flannery O'Connor are reprinted
with the permission of Farrar, Straus & Giroux, Inc., from the
following titles: *Everything That Rises Must Converge,* copyright © 1956, 1957, 1958, 1960, 1961, 1962, 1965 by the Estate
of Mary Flannery O'Connor. From *The Violent Bear It Away,*
copyright © 1955, 1960 by Flannery O'Connor. From *Wise
Blood,* copyright © 1949, 1952, 1962 by Flannery O'Connor.
And from *Mystery and Manners,* edited by Sally and Robert
Fitzgerald, copyright © 1957, 1961, 1963, 1964, 1966, 1967,
1969 by the Estate of Mary Flannery O'Connor. Copyright ©
1962 by Flannery O'Connor, copyright © 1961 by Farrar, Straus
& Cudahy, Inc.

Excerpts from *A Good Man Is Hard to Find and Other Stories,*
copyright © 1953, 1954, 1955 by Flannery O'Connor, are reprinted with the permission of Harcourt Brace Jovanovich, Inc.

I also wish to thank the editors of *Renascence* for material
which originally appeared in my article "*The Violent Bear It
Away:* Moral and Dramatic Sense" (Volume 22, Number 1,
Autumn 1969), copyright © Catholic Renascence Society, and
the editor of the *Georgia Review* for permission to use parts of
my essay "The City of Woe: Flannery O'Connor's Dantean
Vision" (Volume 23, Number 2, Summer 1969), copyright 1969
by the University of Georgia.

Contents

Preface		*vii*
Chapter One	The Landscape of the Grotesque	*1*
Chapter Two	The Grotesque Protagonist	*19*
Chapter Three	Grotesque Action: The Metaphor of Journey	*51*
Chapter Four	Violence and the Grotesque	*76*
Chapter Five	The Catholic Grotesque	*99*
Notes		*115*
Index		*122*

To Laleh

Preface   I have been told that Flannery O'Connor read *The Pooh Perplex* with glee, and that subsequently she referred to the act of criticism as the perplex business. Given Miss O'Connor's skepticism about the value of criticism, I can scarcely offer any justification for yet another study of her own work; probably the only consolation that she would have found in the present exercise in confusion lies in the fact that it is brief.

Miss O'Connor liked to term herself a realist of distances, by which she meant that she wanted to extend reality outward until it embraced religious mystery—an exercise that is unfashionable in literature these days. Admittedly religious mystery is somewhat shapeless for all of us, but Flannery O'Connor managed to capture its lines and color better than any American artist since Hawthorne, a writer whom she admired inordinately. Her success in grasping this area of mystery depended, to a large extent, on her ability literally to shock the reader into acknowledging the spiritual core of her fiction by creating some of the most outrageous protagonists and most improbable action in contemporary fiction. The consistency of practice in her work is striking, and her use of the Catholic grotesque as vision and technique serves, I think, to define the essence of her fiction.

In order to illuminate the Catholic grotesque there has been a necessary exclusion or diminution of secondary themes and attitudes in Miss O'Connor's fiction, but despite these omissions I trust that my thesis remains sound.

If it is, part of the success belongs to certain individuals who contributed their time and advice to this project. I owe clear debts to Alfred Appel, Jr., of Northwestern University, who generously shared his insights on the grotesque with me; to Lawrence Ryan of Stanford University, who closely examined the entire text, especially my treatment of the theological groundings of Miss O'Connor's fiction; and to Richard Scowcroft of Stanford University, who helped me to refine my analysis of Miss O'Connor's novels.

Above all I am indebted to my wife, who has counseled and foreborn, and who graciously spent countless weekends in the company of large and startling figures.

·◦❦ The Landscape of the Grotesque ❧◦·

Chapter One   Flannery O'Connor once remarked that the most memorable event in her life prior to the publication of *Wise Blood* was the featuring of a bantam chicken which she had trained to walk backwards by Pathé newsreels. Mary Flannery was six years old at the time, attending parochial school in Savannah, Georgia. Later, while enrolled at Peabody High School in Milledgeville, where the family had moved in 1938, she confounded her home economics teacher by outfitting another bantam hen in a white piqué coat and striped trousers which she had designed and sewn to specification. Up to the time of her death in 1964 at the age of thirty-nine, Miss O'Connor retained this fondness for domestic fowl, especially those varieties which were eccentric rather than normative. She even confessed to favoring barnyard birds "with one green eye and one orange or with overlong necks and crooked combs. I wanted one with three legs or three wings but nothing in that line turned up."[1]

Unable to locate her ideal grotesque among God's humbler creatures, Miss O'Connor turned to her fellow human beings. And here she discovered a Goyaesque assortment of deformed individuals which she made as unique and imperishable as her bantam hens. In dealing with these human grotesques, the author was writing from personal and drastic experience; she lived in a region where Bible Belt values strongly affected both culture and the human will. Moreover, Miss O'Connor's own affliction, which she carried with her during the major part of her literary career, forced a certain austerity upon her fiction; inevitably she transferred personal agony and suffering to her work. Yet in dealing with her characters' agonies, and in sustaining her own, Flannery O'Connor was sardonic rather than sentimental. She wielded a literary hatchet rather than a handkerchief; she realized that only a stern intellect, an adamant faith, and an accretion of humor which usually shaded into the grotesque could confront suffering, violence, and evil in this world.

In the fictive landscape which she created, Flannery O'Connor's grotesques—deformed in body and soul alike —wrangle with ultimate problems which also must have beset their creator. Her use of the grotesque to establish the moral and aesthetic climate of a work is pronounced, but it is not, as William Van O'Connor has suggested, a peculiarly modern method.[2] Actually the tradition of the grotesque has many antecedents. Viewed historically, the aesthetic is older than its designation: the noted German art historian Wolfgang Kayser cites presences of the grotesque in the convolutions of early Roman art, despite the fact that the term, *la grottesca,* was not applied to these manifestations until the late fifteenth century.[3] Properly speaking, however, the grotesque first became prominent during the Middle Ages. A grotesque perspective was frequently offered by church art, which revealed to a contemporary of these times, Saint Bernard of Clairvaux, "a wonderful sort of hideous beauty and beautiful deformity."[4] Moreover, numerous analogies to the grotesque can be found in medieval graphic art, where comedy is often allied with the more somber aspects of the fantastic, the hallucinatory, and the terrible.

When Gothic form (which should not be confused with the later literary development of Gothic romance) replaced its Romanesque predecessor in the twelfth century, the evolution of the grotesque actually became unavoidable; with fixed proportions destroyed and replaced by spatial distortions and increasingly complex forms, the groundwork had been established for an art of the grotesque. Most importantly, High Gothic form reveals a profound sense of contrast and contradiction in impulses and relationships, as though things are always on the verge of disintegration. As Erwin Panofsky accurately describes it, the key to this period is found in an "ACCEPTANCE AND ULTIMATE RECONCILIATION OF CONTRADICTORY POSSIBILITIES."[5] In viewing the proliferation of contradictory aspects in fourteenth-century art—in roof bosses, stained glass, wood carving, wall painting, and the marginalia of manuscripts—we can readily perceive that High Gothic form, characterized by this juxtaposition of extremes, nurtured in itself an aesthetic which eventually found expression in the pure grotesque.

The late fourteenth century produced one of the fore most artists of the pure grotesque, a figure extremely relevant to this inquiry, because the eschatological themes of Hieronymus Bosch, concerned with Heaven and Hell, the Last Judgment, and the Deadly Seven, are similar in many respects to the main literary preoccupations of Flannery O'Connor. In fact, Bosch's most famous painting, the *Millennium* triptych, provides a gloss on what Miss O'Connor termed her "stories of original sin." Reading from left to right, the three panels of the *Millennium* show how evil came into the world, how it spread through Creation, and how it inevitably leads to Hell. Yet when the panels are closed, one is presented with an ordered view of the universe on the third day of Creation. Like Bosch, Flannery O'Connor creates a landscape wherein life is already hellish, and where men are possessed by demons and devils who completely control their souls and who subject them to excruciating torment.

Her own Millennium canvas, dominated by the unexpected and disconnected, the malformed and the estranged, projects what is perhaps the most consistently grotesque body of work in our time. What both Bosch and Miss O'Connor present, in a style that is pointed and precise, is a violation of the limits which have been laid down by God for man. Thus, for these two artists, the grotesque does not function gratuitously, but in order to reveal underlying and essentially theological concepts.

The contemporary grotesque has predecessors not only in the visual arts but in literature as well, for the popular verbal fun and macabre wit which we encounter in Rabelais and Swift, the demented souls and retarded fools in many of Shakespeare's plays, the Dickensian caricatures and Dostoevskian madmen who populate late nineteenth- and twentieth-century fiction are facets in a continuous and rather pervasive literary aesthetic which scholars have yet to define adequately. Within the restricted province of American literature the grotesque has been an informing principle. It has its genesis in the autobiographical writing of the colonial period, where gross exaggeration of flora and fauna, as well as absurd contortions of faith, are casually remarked. There are aspects of the grotesque in the fiction of Charles Brockden Brown and Poe, writers who generally rely on the trappings of Gothic romance but who, in revealing a merging of categories, a preoccupation with subjective states of being, and a comic tone in face of the terrible, create a tension more readily associated with the grotesque. The grotesque also provides a dark current in an astonishing body of southwestern humor which extends from the 1830s well into the Genteel Age, where it was picked up by writers like Ambrose Bierce and carried into the twentieth century. In the opening decades of the twentieth century Sherwood Anderson gave the

grotesque a certain poetic substance, and F. Scott Fitzgerald, in parts of *The Great Gatsby* and in the middle
section of *The Vegetable,* recognized excrescences of it
in the Jazz Age. Among the major writers of the thirties
the grotesque was a seminal impulse in the fiction of
Faulkner and Nathanael West; and it continues to per-
vade the best contemporary fiction, for to examine such
writers as Vladimir Nabokov, John Barth, James Purdy,
John Hawkes, and Thomas Pynchon—all of whom emphasize the personal vagaries of insanity and the contradictory impulses of identity in conflict with a world that
is essentially chaotic and absurd—is to realize that these
writers accept the grotesque as a matter of course.[6]
   Essentially the grotesque in literature is a method of
investigating certain metaphysical problems through
fictive constructions. In other words the grotesque projects a world vision that is framed by distinct techniques:
in the best grotesque art, vision and technique must function congruently. The vision itself presents existence as
deprived of meaning. All traces of natural order are will-
fully subverted so as to produce an alienated world, a
world in which man, sensing the radical discontinuity of
things, is estranged from his environment. This division
between man and his environment is what actually produces the grotesque, or the absurd, wherein man discovers that in a universe which is disjointed and senseless, which is contradictory in every aspect, he is
something less than what he should be. Camus correctly
calls this division between man and his world, a "divorce," underscoring the concept by remarking that "the
feeling of absurdity does not spring from the mere scrutiny of a fact or an impression, but it . . . bursts from the
comparison of a bare fact and a certain reality, between
an action and the world that transcends it."[7]
   To the extent that both words refer to the alienated

world, we can say that the grotesque and the absurd are synonymous. Wolfgang Kayser, whose definition still remains the best in modern criticism, states that the grotesque is predicated upon this alienated vision, upon what he terms

THE ESTRANGED WORLD . . . . Suddenness and surprise are essential elements . . . . We are so strongly affected and terrified because it is our world which ceases to be reliable, and we feel that we would be unable to live in this changed world. The grotesque instills the fear of life rather than the fear of death. Structurally, it presupposes that the categories which apply to our world view become inapplicable. We have observed the progressive dissolution . . . the fusion of realms which we know to be separated, the abolition of the law of statics, the loss of identity, the distortion of "natural" size and shape, the suspension of the category of objects, the destruction of the personality, and the fragmentation of the historical order . . . . THE GROTESQUE IS A PLAY WITH THE ABSURD . . . . AN ATTEMPT TO INVOKE AND SUBDUE THE DEMONIC ASPECTS OF THE WORLD.[8]

Kayser's analysis suggests that the grotesque is a literature of extreme situation, and indeed mayhem, chaos, and violence seem to predominate in the genre, causing characters to be projected in curious ways. As the world disintegrates and categories merge, these characters frequently become burlesque figures whose actions mime the grotesque world which they inhabit.

The grotesque character therefore is one who either exerts himself against the absurd or who is a part of the absurd. This character frequently assumes recognizable postures: guilt, obsession, and madness are among his peculiarities, and at his best he is simultaneously a rebel, rogue, and victim. He can also be prankster, saint, demonist, fanatic, clown, moron, or any combination of these; or at the more mundane level the grotesque can be reflected in an absurd family group. All these types appear in Flannery O'Connor's gallery of grotesques — and others as well, for as Miss O'Connor was fond of remarking, we are all grotesques in one aspect or another, although we might not realize it; since what most people consider to be normal is actually grotesque, whereas the grotesque itself, because of its pervasiveness, is merely reality.

The grotesque character is a comic figure. It is impossible to sympathize with him, despite his agonies, because we view him from a detached perspective, and when we are not emotionally involved in his suffering, we are amused. Martin Esslin, in examining the theater of the absurd, stresses this principle when he writes:

> Characters with whom the audience fails to identify are inevitably comic. If we identified with the figure of farce who loses his trousers, we should feel embarrassment and shame. If, however, our tendency to identify has been inhibited by making such a character grotesque, we laugh at his predicament. We see what happens to him from the outside, rather than from his own point of view.[9]

As with the grotesque character the entire technique of the grotesque is also essentially comic, for we always view the grotesque from a vantage point. To be certain, the subject matter of the grotesque — the raw material which creates the vision — is always potentially horrible, but the treatment of this material is comic: this explains the peculiar complexity of tone, combining both horror and the ludicrous, which characterizes the grotesque as an art form. Pure horror, of course, cannot produce a grotesque effect: as subject matter it is unrelieved horror and nothing more. But the grotesque, through the interjection of humor, releases the terror and makes it understandable. It is perhaps legitimate to speak of a comic grotesque as distinguished from a "black" grotesque, but it is more precise to say that the grotesque is always a source of humor. (Baudelaire's definition of the grotesque as "the absolute comic" stresses this criterion.) And usually the final equilibrium of the grotesque consists of amused introspection, although to qualify Esslin, we are prevented from laughing at the characters with an easy conscience because of the grotesque's deliberate play upon matters of life and death.

The major comic technique utilized by the writer of the grotesque is exaggeration, and this method inheres in the genre in several ways. One of the most common applications of exaggeration can be located in deformity. When treated in perspective, deformity does not necessarily partake of exaggeration. But when the writer magnifies it beyond normal proportions, when manifestations of the deformed are deliberately enlarged and exploded, then a heightened variety of distortion is created which is amenable to the grotesque. As with the element of horror deformity in itself is not grotesque; it must be exaggerated, and it tends more readily toward the grotesque in those instances where there is a distinct combination of horror and comic fascination, a humorous yet at the same time relieved detachment from the object of deformity.

The value of the deformed to a theory of the grotesque lies precisely in the power to attract and repel concurrently, in the tension which it creates between the conflicting elements involved. Flannery O'Connor properly understood the contradictory impulses which arise when deformed objects are accentuated, and she frequently employed this method in her fiction. One excellent example of the tension implicit in this aspect of the grotesque can be found in Miss O'Connor's short story "The Lame Shall Enter First" (1962), where the author describes various prosthetic devices which the social worker Sheppard and the club-footed boy Rufus encounter: "The brace shop was a small concrete warehouse lined and stacked with the equipment of affliction. Wheel chairs and walkers covered most of the floor. The walls were hung with every kind of crutch and brace. Artificial limbs were stacked on the shelves, legs and arms and hands, claws and hooks, straps and human harnesses and unidentifiable instruments of unnamed deformities."[10] These objects, which are inherently horrible and deformed, are actually designed to correct deformity; and it remains for Rufus, in his comic rebellion against them, to bring the full force of the grotesque to the surface of the story.

Another variety of exaggeration which is pervasive in the grotesque is melodrama, a form of heightened action, frequently comic, which relies upon suddenness, surprise, and shock. Many of Miss O'Connor's stories (for example, the conclusions of "A Good Man is Hard to Find" and "A Late Encounter With the Enemy") strikingly illustrate the value of exaggerated action. Although many of her endings are melodramatically surprising, they are also ridiculous and horrible; thus the magnification of action through melodrama can easily result in a grotesque effect, which is to say that the melodramatic convention, so frequently maligned, has a valuable place in any general theory of the grotesque.

Miss O'Connor appreciated the value of exaggeration as an adjunct of the grotesque. Speaking of her second novel, *The Violent Bear It Away*, she remarked:

When I write a novel in which the central action is baptism, I have to assume that for the general reader, or the general run of readers, baptism is a meaningless rite, and I have to arrange the action so that this baptism carries enough awe and terror to jar the reader into some kind of emotional recognition of its significance. I have to make him feel, viscerally if no other way, that something is going on here that counts. Distortion is an instrument in this case; exaggeration has its purpose.[11]

Emphasis upon the stark outlines of her fiction also caused Flannery O'Conner to utilize exaggeration in the development of character. The simplest form of character exaggeration is name humor, a type of caricature that frequently establishes a comic rhythm partaking of the incongruous, the irrational, and the mechanical aspects of the grotesque. In her fiction Miss O'Connor invents a virtual directory of names which suggest ambiguities, contradictions, and obsessions. Among the more memorable characters who are thus caricatured are Tom T. Shiftlet, the shifty and shiftless prankster in "The Life You Save May Be Your Own," and his prospective mother-in-law, Lucynell Crater, whose name reflects a wasteland environment; Mr. Paradise, a pig-like incarnation of the devil who, in "The River," offers the boy Bevel the hope of false salvation; Joy Hopewell, the cynical and atheistic cripple in "Good Country People," who by the end of the story is berefit of joy, hope, and well-being; and Haze Motes, the prototypical grotesque hero of *Wise Blood*, whose befogged vision is corrected only through the blaze of crucifixion. Caricature, whether in the form of name humor or broad stereotype, is properly grotesque, for it gets at the heart of absurd reality, while simultaneously heightening aspects of it.

A more complicated form of grotesque caricature relies upon a technique which traditionally has been a major phenomenon of the genre, namely the fusion of the animate and inanimate, the human and non-human. This fusion of disparate objects places characters in a world where the laws of symmetry and proportion no longer obtain, where normal actions and reactions break down. The mother in "A Good Man Is Hard to Find," whose face "was as broad and innocent as a cabbage and was tied around with a green headkerchief that had two points on top like rabbit's ears," suggests such grotesque fusion, as does Mrs. Freeman, the tenant in "Good Country People," whose three expressions—forward, neutral, and reverse—transform her into an automaton.

Just as human beings are reduced to the grotesque postures of animals and inanimate objects, it is natural that the inanimate and non-human can partake of the human, because the fusion of categories can operate from a variety of positions. Thus the black valise of the grandmother in "A Good Man Is Hard to Find" resembles the head of a hippopotamus, while the tractor in "A View of the Woods" gorges on clay like a human being. Moreover, this contingency of objects upon each other can be expanded from an isolated image to a pervasive setting: for example, the stairwell in "A Stroke of Good Fortune" becomes animated, human, and decidedly hostile in the mind of the pregnant Ruby Hill.

With its emphasis upon distortion, melodrama, caricature, and fusion it is readily apparent that grotesque technique is essentially non-realistic, although in terms of the vision it is designed to project it says a great deal about the reality of man's condition. But the realistic tradition, characterized by a subtle delineation of psychological behavior and by proper motivation, by objective reportage of the external world and insistence upon cause and effect, is in many ways antithetical to the grotesque, which utilizes different methods of evaluating "reality," while never excluding realism as one of many possibilities.

The grotesque is also distinct from the conventions of romance, especially those which we associate with Gothic fiction. Although several critics have attempted to establish a variety of modern Gothic fiction to which Flannery O'Connor belongs, they are confusing genres and using language loosely,[12] since there are considerable differences between the two conventions. Gothic fiction, whether traditional or modern, is a variety of romance which dwells upon imaginative terror in order to create a special atmosphere. Rather than comedy and terror, which are combined in the grotesque, we encounter suspense and terror in the Gothic; and, of course, to the modern reader Gothic fiction is frequently ludicrous, but this is never consciously intended. Isolated and picturesque settings, beautiful heroines and noble sentiments, marked by a tone of melancholy and awe, serve to define Gothic romance and to remove it as a genre from the grotesque. Moreover, Gothic romance does not project a valid world vision as does the grotesque: it merely assaults the nerves by making us believe in the horror of the supernatural, whereas the grotesque forces metaphysical problems upon the intellect.

When Mrs. Radcliffe, in her preface to *The Italian*, described the ability of Gothic romance to transcend the dull truths of the earth and to soar after new wonders into a world of its own, she inadvertently provided today's critics with a key to the genesis of a modern variety of romance which utilizes Gothic trappings, namely surrealism. When he praised the English Gothic novel in his 1924 *Manifeste du surréalisme*, André Breton was seemingly aware of the affinities between Gothic romance and his movement: essentially, both genres glorify the marvelous and imbue it with an aura of beauty in a manner totally alien to the grotesque. But to view the paintings of Giorgio de Chirico, Yves Tanguy, and Salvador Dali, with their combinations of disparate objects, their preoccupation with the irrational, and their curious varieties of humor, is to recognize that in terms of technique there are resemblances between the surrealistic and grotesque modes of art.[13] Yet only surrealism embraces a purely Gothic approach to romantic materials; just as the Gothic espouses the primacy of terror, surrealism espouses the primacy of nightmare and of the imagination in general by using such essentially Gothic methods as visions, hallucinations, alchemy, magic, and the primitive.

Not only does surrealism rely on romanticism's more unfortunate aspects as revealed in the Gothic mode, but its distrust of the rational leads to a glorification of the irrational, an effect rarely attempted by the grotesque, which merely tries to present the irrational as one aspect of its vision of the world, but not as an end in itself. In fact surrealism, a degraded romantic aesthetic, never manages to project a philosophical world view in the manner of the grotesque. Circumscribed as it is by mystery, fantasy, and dream, surrealism pursues other and less substantial chimeras of reality — and for different purposes — than the grotesque.

In the final analysis the grotesque is neither romantic nor realistic but an aesthetic unique in itself. To a large extent this explains why, during the decade of the fifties, critics of Miss O'Connor's work, bereft of familiar genres, were perplexed and disoriented by the grotesque ambience of her fiction. They variously regarded her as a writer of Gothic romance, as the arch priestess of "the cult of the gratuitous grotesque," and as a Roman Catholic Erskine Caldwell. At their worst, unable to comprehend the essential genius of her fiction, they contented themselves by emulating the procedure of a certain *Time* reviewer who analyzed Miss O'Conner's short stories by extracting blurbs from the dust jackets of her books. Flannery O'Connor was never uncertain of the tenor of her fiction. She thought that men were necessarily involved in a world which is inherently grotesque and that as a Catholic her perception of the terror and ludicrousness of life was best explained in theological terms. Her first story, entitled "The Geranium," was written a year before she was graduated from the University of Iowa in 1947 with a master of fine arts degree, and it reveals generically the major concerns which were to preoccupy her in the two novels and twenty-one short stories which she was subsequently to write. Although "The Geranium" is not representative of Miss O'Connor's best fiction (she once admitted that she presented herself to Paul Engle without knowing a short story from a newspaper advertisement), it contains several aspects of the grotesque which are worth examining. To begin with, the landscape of the tale is properly grotesque: in casting her central figure, a displaced Southerner, in an alien metropolitan setting, the author creates an environment which is decidedly hostile and foreboding. To Old Dudley, the city is like a nightmare, and thus his physical environment becomes an effective index of his spiritual condition. In such passages as the following one, we can detect the sort of profound alienation from one's environment which Camus describes as the hallmark of the grotesque:

> New York was swishing and jamming one minute and dirty and dead the next. His daughter didn't even live in a house. She lived in a building—the middle of a row of buildings all alike, all blackened—red and gray with rasp-mouthed people hanging out their windows and other people just like them looking back. Inside you could go up and you could go down and there were just halls that reminded you of tape measures

strung out with a door every inch. He remembered he'd been dazed by the building the first week. He'd wake up expecting the halls to have changed in the night and he'd look out the door and there they stretched like dog runs. The streets were the same way. He wondered where he'd be if he walked to the end of one of them. One night he dreamed he did and ended at the end of the building—nowhere.[14]

This paragraph has the impact of much grotesque visual art. Indeed, it is strongly reminiscent of a painting by A. Paul Weber entitled *The Rumor*, in which hordes of grotesque people hang out of windows in postures reduplicating Miss O'Connor's image of the "rasp-mouthed people." From the time that she submitted cartoons and lithographs to her high school literary magazine and yearbook, Miss O'Connor maintained an interest in the visual arts, and this explains why in her application of the grotesque she is so strongly aligned with artists like the early Roualt, and with the tradition of Gothic religion painting from Grünewald on down to Ensor. She is by far the most graphic of postwar American writers.

The geranium, which is placed on the window sill every morning to catch the sun, reminds Old Dudley of the far superior geraniums grown in the South and of a certain Grisby boy, the first in a long line of O'Connor grotesques, "who had polio and had to be wheeled out every morning and left in the sun to blink" (p. 245). To the extent that Dudley's urban plight has a certain reality of embodiment, he too is a minor grotesque, but his behavior and actions lack the comic intensity of method which characterizes Miss O'Connor's most effective construction of grotesque individuals. This fact, combined with the obvious and rather simplistic symbol of the geranium, with the character of a stereotyped Negro servant who is little more than the embodiment of Nigger Jim, and with a conclusion which simply diffuses without contributing to the implications of the story, suggests an immature talent at work, but a talent far from juvenile, since Flannery O'Connor was already attempting to formulate a grotesque vision—and to develop the appropriate techniques for conveying it.

Just before her death Miss O'Connor revised "The Geranium" and retitled it "Judgment Day" (1965). In the revised story her conception of human nature, of good and evil, and of their relation to the grotesque is much deeper and much more complex than in the original. Tanner, the old man in "Judgment Day," is an avatar of Old Dudley: he resembles his earlier counterpart in that he too finds himself estranged from his native roots and forced to live in an alien metropolis. But he transcends Dudley's dimensions of character in that he is obsessed with ultimate things, with what his atheistic daughter terms " 'morbid stuff, death and hell and judgment.' " Here also is a spiritual conflict to reckon with that was largely absent in "The Geranium." Even Tanner's dreams mirror these theological preoccupations: in one recurring dream his corpse is being transported home; and as it reaches its destination, his friends hear a scratching noise, and when the coffin lid is pried open, Tanner leaps out, shouting "Judgment Day, Judgment Day."

It is the opposition between what is serious and potentially terrifying—and Miss O'Connor's comic treatment of this material—which creates the grotesque flavor of the tale. Tanner is leaving New York because he has overheard his daughter telling her husband that she is going to bury the old man in a New York plot after he is dead. Tanner is determined to see that he gets buried in the South. Prior to his departure he has pinned a note in his pocket: "IF FOUND DEAD SHIP TO COLEMAN PARRUM, CORINTH, GEORGIA." And when he looks at his daughter, his eyes are "trained on her like the eyes of an angry corpse." Thus, by rendering death in various postures of the absurd, Miss O'Connor places Tanner's will in oposition to the climax of the story; and this opposition between intention and reality illuminates a major aspect of the grotesque.

Tanner dies before he can begin his journey home, and his daughter discovers him on the landing of the stairs: "his hat had been pulled down over his face and his head and arms thrust between the spoke of the banisters; his feet dangled over the stairwell like those of a man in stocks." With his crucifixion etched in the acid of the grotesque, as are the real and ritualistic crucifixions of other O'Connor characters (such as Guizac in "The Displaced Person," Haze Motes in *Wise Blood*, and Parker in "Parker's Back"), Tanner demonstrates clearly the ability of the grotesque to render character in complicated postures which simultaneously evoke the effects of terror and the ludicrous.

Tanner's abortive journey thus creates a minor allegory which records the tragic implications of man's fate in a world deprived of meaning. Miss O'Connor relies upon a religious conception of nature to explain the accumulation of the grotesque in this world; and God's judgment certainly is involved in the fact that sin, suffering, and infirmity were brought into the world following the Fall. A connection can be established between existential dislocation, which is at the core of the grotesque vision, and spiritual dissociation: this explains why most of Miss O'Connor's characters can be evaluated by their attitude toward Christianity.

All men, Flannery O'Connor realized, must eventually embark on a trip similar to Tanner's. This metaphor of voyage actually defines a substantial amount of grotesque action in her fiction. These voyages inevitably culminate in suffering, evil, and disorder—with many of those forces which reinforce a grotesque vision. Miss O'Connor, however, goes beyond many writers of what we might term the secular grotesque by invoking religion as a way of confronting the absurd. As Kayser remarks, a true art of the grotesque not only reveals but also subdues the demonic. If O'Connor utilizes Catholic values to arrive at certain truths about the grotesque, it is because she wants to provide a corrective to man's desperate and meaningless condition by emphasizing the theological foundations of nature and grace.

In promulgating an antidote to the absurd, Flannery O'Connor creates what properly should be termed an art of the Catholic grotesque. She manuevers her characters through dark and inpenetrable mazes which seemingly lead nowhere, but which unexpectedly reveal an exit into Christianity's back yard. While she affirms the contradictory aspects of the universe, her fiction nevertheless embodies a transcending principle of order. For Miss O'Connor spiritual vitality lies precisely in the strength of the antithesis between the negative aspects of the grotesque and the affirmation of religion: it is between these extremes that she paints her Catholic landscape of the grotesque.

The Grotesque Protagonist

Chapter Two In a brief reminiscence the distinguished southern writer Andrew Lytle recalls the first
time that he encountered the reserved young lady who
frequented Paul Engle's fiction workship in the late
1940s:

> Years ago at Iowa City in a rather informal class meeting I
> read aloud a story by one of the students. I was told later
> that it was understood that I would know how to pronounce
> in good country idiom the word chitling which appeared in
> the story. At once it was obvious that the author of the story
> was herself not only Southern but exceptionally gifted. The
> idiom for her characters rang with all the truth of the real
> thing, but the real thing heightened. . . . I realized that what
> she had done was what any first rate artist always does — she
> had made something more essential than real life but
> resembling it.[1]

This episode transcends the anecdotal, because Lytle
seems to be examining the relationship of fiction to life.
He recognizes that the main principle involved in any
mimetic theory of art is the angle of the writer's vision to
life, and in the case of Flannery O'Connor he discovered
that this mimetic angle produced an effect of extreme intensity and concentration. Lytle's evaluation of the tenor
of Miss O'Connor's fiction is accurate; even in her early
work, and especially in *Wise Blood*, which was started
under Engle's tutelage in 1947, her materials do not
duplicate life as a photograph would, but rather approach
it from a heightened perspective.

As Flannery O'Connor wrote and revised *Wise Blood*, first at Iowa City, then at Yaddo, and finally in New York City (where in 1949 she began an abiding friendship with Robert and Sally Fitzgerald), she must have been aware of the extreme perspective presented in that novel. To be certain the literature which she was reading at the time dovetailed with her own methods and themes. The most pervasive influence in *Wise Blood* is that of Nathanael West. As Stanley Edgar Hyman first observed: "Hazel Motes has a nose 'like a shrike's bill'; after he goes to bed with Leora Watts, Haze feels 'like something washed ashore on her'; Sabbath Lilly's correspondence with a newspaper advice-columnist is purest West; and all the rocks in *Wise Blood* recall the rock Miss Lonelyhearts first contains in his gut and then becomes, the rock on which the new Peter will found the new Church."[2] Resemblances between the two books exceed those enumerated by Hyman. Four of the fourteen chapters in *Wise Blood* appeared as short stories between 1948 and 1952, and in one of them, "The Peeler," Asa Hawks is called Asa Shrike. Throughout the first half of Miss O'Connor's frequently reworked novel this ostensibly blind fanatic is the main adversary of Haze Motes, just as Shrike is the scourge of Miss Lonelyhearts. Moreover, the very fact that the chapters in *Wise Blood* are self-contained episodes suggests a basic structural similarity with West's book; both rely on the frame technique of the comic strip, a method that the author quite possibly adapted from her experience as a college cartoonist.

The original form of *Wise Blood* can only be guessed, but the extent of revision can be gauged by the six typewritten pages of suggested changes made to Miss O'Connor by her friend and mentor, Caroline Gordon. The preponderance of visual imagery in the novel, for instance, is probably a late addition, and one that grew out of her reading of *Oedipus Rex* while she was at work on the manuscript. Furthermore, the pervasiveness of coffin imagery, the preoccupation with grotesque postures of death, and the highly fluctuating point of view closely parallel Faulkner's method in *As I Lay Dying*, which was one of Miss O'Connor's favorite novels.

The moral vision of writers like West, Sophocles, and Faulkner was obviously congenial to Flannery O'Connor, because she found her natural idiom in stories where the characters—Miss Lonelyhearts, Oedipus, the Bundrens—confront the limits of mystery. As Miss O'Connor once remarked in delineating her own work, "the look of this fiction is going to be wild . . . it is almost of necessity going to be violent and comic, because of the discrepancies that it seeks to combine."[3] And the writer who cultivates this type of vision, based on characters "who are forced out to meet evil and grace and who act on a trust beyond themselves,"[4] will inevitably be interested in the grotesque.

Miss O'Connor began writing about grotesques because she could, as she readily admitted in a letter to James Farnham, recognize them. "Essentially the reason why my characters are grotesque," she explained, "is because it is the nature of my talent to make them so. To some extent the writer can choose his subject; but he can never choose what he is able to make live. It is characters like the Misfit and the Bible salesman that I can make live."[5] Flannery O'Connor was pre-eminently successful in character depiction because she realized that the grotesque was the ideal vehicle for objectifying fears, obsessions, and compulsions. Within her southern landscape (only two of her stories are set outside the South, and they involve southern characters), it is the common everyday confrontations, such as a family trip or a visit to the doctor's office, that are filled with horror, and it is the sudden irrationality of the familiar world that induces distortions in character. Thus the grotesque suggests that the visible world is incomprehensible and unregenerate, and that the individual is floundering in a sea of contradictions and incongruities.

The typical grotesque character in Miss O'Connor's fiction is an individual who projects certain extreme mental states which, while psychologically valid, are not investigations in the tradition of psychological realism. To be certain, the reality of the unconscious life — incorporating dream, fantasy, and hallucination — is expressed, but grotesque characterization is not interested in the subtleties of emotion and feeling, but rather in their larger outlines. This method actually tends toward the symbolic, where distillation of character into a basic set of preoccupations serves to crystallize attitudes toward the ethical circumstances being erected. Here a basic point to emphasize is that grotesque characterization does not necessarily make the characters in a story remote or improbable, since the sacrifice in psychological realism is more counterbalanced by the impact of the grotesque. For instance, it is clearly evident in O'Connor's fiction that boldly outlined inner compulsions are reinforced dramatically by a mutilated exterior self, as with Tom T. Shiftlet in "A Good Man is Hard to Find," Hulga in "Good Country People," and Rufus in "The Lame Shall Enter First." Moreover, these compulsions are frequently projected into the surrounding environment: in "A Circle in the Fire," for example, Mrs. Cope ironically conceives of the farm as an image of her own indomitable nature, as an extension of her own creation; and in "A View of the Woods" there is a deliberate effort to link the obsessions of the main character, Mr. Fortune, with the landscape, which is frequently rendered through terse, unpleasant, and decidedly violent imagery.

In effect the grotesque character is "demonic," and as such he certainly embraces as wide a moral range as characters created through the techniques of psychological realism. Frequently the grotesque protagonist is fated, obsessed, driven by his demon. Historically he has been preoccupied with problems of temptation, sin, guilt, and expiation. His actions are highly stylized and arc at times ambivalent, because to him causality does not exist. He is "flat" to the extent that he is obsessed, that he is automaton-like, that his compulsive gestures are mechanical. He speaks to us universally, except in those instances of the impure grotesque where writers are working out special preoccupations: Truman Capote's haunted characters, for example, and those of Tennessee Williams, frequently seem to derive from a personal context that is not totally relevant to the wider vision of the grotesque. With O'Connor, however, the grotesque character is never gratuitous; he speaks to us about our own experience, and he responds to a world that has recognizable attributes.

Thus the grotesque character is not necessarily a simple creation. Just how complicated he can be is apparent in *Wise Blood*, in which Haze Motes is presented as the epitome of the grotesque protagonist. Haze is a young man who is continually buffeted by the incredible, by the essence of the grotesque vision of the world. But with Motes we are dealing with many interrelated aspects of personality, any one of which can function exclusively as a grotesque type. Haze is many men simultaneously: fanatic, demonist, rogue, clown, and Christ figure; displaced by the war, he frequently operates at a child's level of intelligence, and he is capable of giving us an animal's view of things.

For the better part of the action Haze's nature is opposed to grace, and this fundamental divorce creates a narrative that is tinged with both nightmare and comedy. O'Connor seemingly adumbrated this point in a preface to the second edition of the novel:

> The book was written with zest and, if possible, it should be read that way. It is a comic novel about a Christian *malgre lui*, and as such, very serious, for all comic novels that are any good must be about matters of life and death. *Wise Blood* was written by an author congenitally innocent of theory, but one with certain preoccupations. That belief in Christ is to some a matter of life and death has been a stumbling block for readers who would prefer to think it a matter of no great consequence. For them Hazel Motes' integrity lies in his trying with such vigor to get rid of the ragged figure who moves from tree to tree in the back of his mind. For the author Hazel's integrity lies in his not being able to. Does one's integrity ever lie in what he is not able to do? I think that usually it does, for free will does not mean one will, but many wills conflicting in one man. Freedom cannot be conceived simply. It is a mystery and one which a novel, even a comic novel, can only be asked to deepen.[6]

Haze is a man with an hereditary obsession: he is congenitally infected—in a manner similar to Francis Marion Tarwater in *The Violent Bear It Away*—with the legacy of his grandfather, a Bible Belt preacher who had traveled three counties, spouting hellfire and brimstone from the hood of a Ford—a car that presages the dilapidated Essex which Haze converts into his house, his pulpit, his justification, and his coffin. Obsessed with Jesus Christ to a degree which precludes normal human behavior, Haze exchanges his black preacher's hat for a white panama, emblematic in O'Connor's fiction of the devil, and he struggles to erect a secular Church without Christ.

It takes most of the novel before Haze learns the innermost secret of his spiritual existence, and at that point where he does discover the core of faith at the center of religious mystery, he blinds himself in atonement for his worldly apostasy. But as a secular prophet obsessed with the baseness of the world, he rebels against being drawn into a theological trap which he initially conceives as a "trick on niggers." This impulse toward the secular is a characteristic affliction of Flannery O'Connor's grotesques, for she sees the modern world divided between those who would eliminate mystery and those who are trying to rediscover it. The secular world which seduces her characters typically divorces eternity from temporality in order to negate the precise area of mystery which Miss O'Connor insists upon. It is a world which values discrete data and the appurtenances of technology, which fragments experience and transforms people into prophets of a new objectivity.

One such prophet is George Rayber, the uncle of Tarwater in *The Violent Bear It Away* (1960), a clinician who tries to save the lad from his baser religious impulses. Rayber is an exponent of existentialist freedom divorced from any concerns of the spirit; but whereas Tarwater eventually accepts grace after a series of violent and cathartic encounters with unmitigated evil, the schoolteacher meets his fate with the empty knowledge that his mechanized spirit has deprived him of grace. His is an ascetic denial of the spirit, an absurd effort to escape from what he, like Haze Motes, conceives to be hereditary madness. That he is alienated from the world is suggested by the grotesque descriptions of his appearance. Tarwater is correct in considering him an automaton, since the metal box he requires to compensate for his deafness is an appendage of himself; his "drill-like eyes" and Tarwater's suspicion that his head runs by electricity reinforce the image of his mechanical nature.

Rayber is a modern freak, a grotesque whose values are undermined by his own inanimate nature. He has counterparts in other stories by O'Connor, most notably in "The Lame Shall Enter First," where Sheppard, the welfare worker, an extreme projection of the militant atheist and scientific objectivist, is forced to admit defeat when confronted with the inexplicable evil of the boy Rufus. Sheppard, who relies on scientific inquiry instead of compassion, is emblematic of the failure of science to satisfy man's basic emotional, psychological, and spiritual needs. He purchases a telescope for the edification of Rufus; but the boy, who is totally alienated from a scientific universe and who adheres to a more traditional world picture, medieval in origin, in which the universe exists between the extremes of heaven and hell, begins to use the telescope for demonic ends. Finally he induces Sheppard's emotionally crippled son to hang himself and thereby launch a trip into space in quest of his deceased mother.

Norton's flight into space, like Rufus Johnson's demonic and violent actions, is not really senseless; in fact it fixes the precise meaning of the story—that the familiar world, illuminated by science, still remains alien and mysterious, even as the source of hope within man's grotesque condition has been known for two thousand years, although that too remains unverifiable. This story, like many others by O'Connor, is a ruthless study of the vulgarity of the secular spirit, a spirit which while assuming such guises as psychology in "The Partridge Festival," art in "The Enduring Chill," and popular culture in "A Late Encounter With the Enemy," more often than not focuses on those manifestations of atheism that are witnessed in Haze Motes, Rayber, and Sheppard.

When Miss O'Connor treats this petrification of spirit, this refusal to believe, she creates a startling malignancy beneath the comic texture of her stories, because atheism never enables grotesque characters to get by in the world that they live in. People are pitted against an overpowering spiritual reality which makes their absurd contortions even more poignant, since it creates an existence so oppressive that individuals literally fall apart. This fact is evident, for instance, in "Good Country People (1955), in which the protagonist, possessing a physiognomy that parallels her distorted spirit, is completely alienated from the world. Hulga, already a victim of certain absur dities, including a shotgun blast which accidentally blew her leg off in childhood, is rendered even more susceptible to the radical discontinuities of existence, despite her impervious façade, because she denies the significance of life and the possibility of immortality. Having taken a Ph.D. in philosophy, she has arrived at an intellectual position, similar to that of Haze, Rayber, and Sheppard, which fuses atheism and nihilism. "If science is right," she underlines in a book which she is reading, "then one thing stands firm: science wishes to know nothing of nothing. Such is after all the strictly scientific approach to Nothing." Belief in such solipsistic nonsense reveals the sort of intellectual pride, found in Hawthorne's fiction as well as O'Connor's, which debases the individual and makes him grotesque.

It requires an encounter with pure evil, embodied in this case in the figure of the demonic Bible salesman, Manly Pointer, to annihilate Hulga's secular dignity. Her grotesque seduction by Pointer destroys her sense of order and deprives her of her philosophic foothold. Intending actually to seduce the Bible salesman, she ironically surrenders first her glasses and then her artificial leg, which constitutes her ultimate sacrifice. This hayloft seduction scene, which is one of the most perfect absurd tableaus in O'Connor's fiction, culminates when Hulga, exposed to extreme evil, suddenly becomes disoriented and reverts to the same platitudes which she had condemned earlier in her mother.

"Good Country People" presents a brilliant and relentless vision of the grotesque, and as such it ranks, along with "The Displaced Person" and "The Artificial Nigger," as one of the finest pieces in Flannery O'Connor's first collection of fiction, *A Good Man is Hard to Find* (1955). Surface illusions are exposed as pretensions, and Hulga's apostasy, at first comic and pathetic, turns with amazing inevitability toward the shocking and uncompromising revelation that her nihilism is worthless when faced with the cold hard presence of evil. This story is a ruthless depiction of an individual, maimed in body and soul, who is subjected to the extreme alienation which comes from the realization that one's entire life is scarcely more than a precarious caricature. Loss of her glasses leaves Hulga symbolically and literally adrift in a world of distorted visions. The extraordinary paradox of the Bible salesman who turns out to be a false Christian and the girl who is exposed as a false atheist is an ideal figure for exposing the grotesque destinies of those myopic souls who have been deprived of grace. Subjected to a situation that is psychologically and morally devastating, Hulga finally learns that she has no identity, and it is at this point in the resolution of the story that she is seized with the horror of the alienated world.

The feverish Bible salesman who applies the genuinely nihilistic lesson to his stunned victim is one of Miss O'Connor's most startling demonic types—a trickster who lacks morals yet who operates within a moral context. This sort of trickster is one of several grotesque types whom we encounter in Flannery O'Connor's fiction. He is a figure (present in her fiction as early as *Wise Blood*) who can be highly contradictory in his impulses and deceptive in his guises, but who always creates disorder through his amoral and destructive actions. In

Wise Blood, for example, most of Haze Motes' avatars, or *doppelgänger*, are rogues who constantly force Haze into untenable and self-destructive situations; yet these tricksters enable Haze to perceive gradually the truth of his situation. Asa Hawks, for one, is a sham prophet—one of several psychological doubles informing Haze's destiny—who pretends blindness and turns religion into a business ethic. Haze, outraged by his commercial travesty upon religion, actually does destroy his eyesight in atonement. Another psychological double who functions as a trickster is Hoover Shoats, alias Onnie Jay Holy, an "artist-type" who attempts to align himself with Motes for financial gain. Unlike Haze he is dressed in a dark suit and white hat; his easy guile and deliberate corruption are outrageous to Motes, who sees in Hoover a grotesque parody of himself. Yet a third psychological double whom Haze must eliminate is the trickster Solace Layfield, a false preacher hired to compete with Motes; eventually Haze kills off the last of his avatars by running him over.

The trickster who functions as a psychological double tends to alienate the central protagonist from the world and from aspects of himself. Especially when the trickster assumes the posture of a clown or fool, he is capable of illuminating those aspects of personality which are absurd or bizarre. Thus in *Wise Blood* much of the plot is organized on the polarity which exists between Haze and his comic counterpart or double, Enoch Emery, a backwoods moron seeking a "new Jesus" who will save him. Enoch, truly without Christ, is a brutal parody of the identity crisis suffered by Motes, who never loses Christ. Like the traditional trickster Enoch is capable of many disguises; however, in a manner typical of the more complicated varieties of tricksters whom we encounter in literature, these disguises seem to rebound upon himself and are thus self-destructive. When Enoch, disguised in a black coat, slanted hat, sunglasses and beard, encounters the gorilla movie star Gonga, he succumbs to a loneliness beyond his comprehension, and the ensuing episode, in which he is insulted by Gonga, who tells him to go to hell, is a comedy of manners with grim, ironic, and decidedly grotesque overtones. It accepts the human condition from the point of view of the dissociated soul and transforms it into something which is irrational, absurd, pathetic, and subhuman. Forced to realize his own failure as a human being, Enoch kills the gorilla impersonator, steals the gorilla suit, and assumes a new animalistic identity. But again the metamorphosis ends in absurd imitation and ridiculous suffering: when Enoch, in his demented happiness, approaches a couple sitting on a hill overlooking the city and extends his hand to greet them, they flee in terror. The scene depicted here is a premonition of a similar revelation which Haze suffers when his car is destroyed; and Enoch's final posture before disappearing—which again foreshadows Haze's stance when he loses his Essex—establishes him as another variety of grotesque double who informs Motes's agony at every point. Enoch's new bestial nature is a revelation of the condition of man without God: all that remains is a pathetic anthropological remnant of man's nobility and capacity for suffering. As an avatar of Haze's central consciousness Enoch, like the other doubles in the novel, performs ridiculous imitations of Haze's religious obsessions; once Haze realizes this, he is quite literally tricked into understanding the hopelessness of his theological inversions.

Thus the grotesque trickster tends to explode surface pretensions in others in order to expose man's absurd condition. The supreme trickster, of course, is the devil, who frequently appears in Flannery O'Connor's fiction wearing a variety of disguises. The Bible salesman, for example, is one of Miss O'Connor's most startling demonic tricksters: his red hands and glittering eyes make him a curiously resonant satanic figure. The benevolent Mr. Paradise in "The River," whose protrusions on his head are a good indication of his origins and his mission, is another incarnation of the devil, as is the mysterious stranger in the white panama hat who continually tempts Tarwater toward sin and damnation in *The Violent Bear It Away*. (A similar figure in a panama hat appears in one of the author's least successful stories, "The Comforts of Home.") These devils are not the sort of disembodied gothic demons associated with tales of the supernatural, but distinct and palpable aspects of existence. "I want to be certain," Miss O'Connor wrote in a letter to John Hawkes, "that the devil gets identified as the devil and not simply taken for this or that psychological tendency."[7] Like Gogol, whom she read assiduously, Flannery O'Connor believed that the devil was a formative influence in life.

When the devil is not present himself in O'Connor's fiction, he nevertheless can exert considerable influence on character behavior. To the extent that her characters are criminal types, they are in the hands of the devil, whether willingly or reluctantly, and by surrendering themselves to infernal forces they commit themselves as well to a grotesque existence. For instance, in "A Good Man is Hard to Find" (1953), Miss O'Connor's memorable antagonist is an astute madman who deliberately places himself in opposition to Christ. The Misfit is cast into a hopeless situation because of the demonic aspects of the world, and his sense of alienation is intensified by his belief that God has abandoned him. What we encounter at the beginning of the story — an absurdly comic narrative of a family trip that is almost a parody of Wilder's "The Happy Journey to Trenton and Camden" — gradually assumes the proportions of a wholesale revolt against the cultural distortions of Christianity.

Preoccupied with the myth of Christ, the Misfit becomes judge and executioner in order to do justice to a social situation in which punishment does not seem to fit the wrong. The Misfit, like it or not, is the religious consciousness of his age. For him the alternatives are simple —belief or disbelief. He chooses the latter course of action, but although he murders all six members of the Bailey family, he doesn't take any pleasure in killing. He murders people because he *wants* to be a sinner in the hands of the devil: he seemingly partakes of Rufus Johnson's premonition that sinners, especially if they repent, are capable of receiving curious dispensations from God. Both Rufus and the Misfit conceive of their criminality in strict theological terms. Both perform their criminal acts for the sake of evil and both consider themselves damned because of them. Yet these criminals do not regard themselves as complete losses because they realize that salvation is a simple matter of repentance, that Jesus is the only one who can save them.

These "criminals" are therefore grotesques of a very special sort. Deliberately cutting themselves off from transcendent values, they lapse into what is essentially an attitude of despair. And with the recession of belief which they experience comes the isolation, alienation, and sense of abandonment that most grotesque protagonists and antagonists feel. This point is strikingly illustrated in one of Miss O'Connor's earlier stories, "The Life You Save May Be Your Own" (1953), where we encounter the black outrageous figure of Tom T. Shiftlet, an individual much more than a criminal—actually a grotesque Christ figure who is decadent and evil. Shiftlet, the one-armed carpenter whose figure forms a crooked cross, marries and abandons a retarded girl in exchange for a dilapidated Ford. What is significant here is that there is an appalling logic and certitude in his actions. Perplexity about his own identity and the mysteries of the human heart drives him to desperate extremities and forces him to investigate demonically the possibilities of evil which arise from his key question—what is man? Shiftlet's self styled "moral intelligence" tells him that man really isn't benevolent, a point which he fully realizes; yet in the inherent potentialities of Shiftlet's moral intelligence for cruelty and evil a statement of the human condition is made which contains the bleak pessimism concerning the moral sense that Mark Twain revealed in *The Mysterious Stranger*.

Tom T. Shiftlet—the trickster who at the end of the story is also tricked—is a grotesque parody of Christ. He cannot save others or even himself. After his abandonment of Lucynell, which constitutes a deliberate act of deception and evil, he encounters road signs which read: "Drive carefully. The life you save may be your own." Yet Shiftlet is unable to comprehend the portent of this message, since any kind of solution to man's infernal condition is beyond his control. By effectively removing himself from grace, he encounters despair and alienation. However, his condition, like that of Rufus and the Misfit, is not entirely hopeless. Miss O'Connor hinted at this when she remarked: "I did have some trouble with the end of that story. I got it up to his taking the girl away and leaving her. I knew I wanted to do that much, and I did it. But the story wasn't complete. I needed that little boy on the side of the road, and that little boy is what makes the story work."[8] When Schlitz Playhouse adapted this story to television, the producer obviously didn't have O'Connor's stricture to serve as a guideline, because he changed the ending completely. "I didn't recognize the television version," commented Miss O'Connor. "Gene

Kelly played Mr. Shiftlet and for the idiot daughter they got some young actress who had just been voted one of the most beautiful women in the world, and they changed the ending just a little bit by having Shiftlet suddenly get a conscience and come back to the girl."[9] Many critics, like the Schlitz people, overlook that little boy. It is he who perceives Shiftlet's hypocrisy, and it is he who makes Shiftlet cognizant of his own evil. Shiftlet, after being abandoned by the boy just as he had deserted Lucynell, suddenly turns inward upon himself and, in a moment of agony, an infinitely small prayer is the only thing he possesses in order to redeem himself. But the astonishing conclusion suggests that salvation first requires a ritualistic purification: "After a few minutes there was a guffawing peal of thunder from behind and fantastic raindrops, like tin-can tops, crashed over the rear of Mr. Shiftlet's car. Very quickly he stepped on the gas and with his stump sticking out of the window he raced the galloping shower into Mobile." Shiftlet in his flight from God's wrath recognizes his own complicity in the face of total estrangement and an impersonal universe which is actively hostile to him. His world is chaotic, and the reader is merely given a glimpse of the antidote to it. A Christ-like life, despite the degradation and perversity that Shiftlet brings to it, somehow remains a mysterious possibility. The anarchy of the finite human situation—and its reconciliation in the religious absolute—finds its grotesque expression in Shiftlet, who affirms negatively the body and symbol of the Catholic tradition.

The distance of Shiftlet from the true Christ represents the dominant experience of our time as interpreted from the viewpoint of the grotesque, insisting as it does upon a fragmentation of man from the world and from common bodies of belief. This fragmentation not only transforms men into cultural and spiritual grotesques, but it also forces new attitudes toward Christ upon the imagination, as Tom T. Shiftlet demonstrates. Another figure who illustrates this point is Guizac, the refugee Pole in "The Displaced Person," a character who, along with Melville's Bartleby, is one of the two most convincing Christ figures in American short fiction. This is an extremely long story running to about 20,000 words. The original version, which appeared in the *Sewanee Review* in 1954, is much shorter and ends with Mrs. Shortley's death; moreover, the full implications of Guizac's figuration as Christ are not developed, the integral peacock symbol does not appear, and the severe emphasis on displacement which characterizes the longer version is not quite so apparent.

In its final form "The Displaced Person" (1955) is divided into three parts, each hinging on a major climax and each centered on the twin symbols of the Displaced Person and the peacock.[10] Mrs. Shortley, who serves as the central consciousness in the first third of the story, perceives the Guizacs as true grotesques. She tends to think of them in non-human terms, likening them to bears, bugs, and monstrous "Gobblehooks." Similarly, in the second part of the story, after Guizac's embodiment of Christ has been effectively established, Mrs. McIntyre, after first considering the refugee Pole as her salvation, finally begins to conceive of him as a monster when she learns of his plan to bring over a cousin in order to marry her to a young Negro. She too now regards Guizac in the metamorphosed aspect of the grotesque, as a pastiche of human and non-human elements: "His forehead and skull were white where they had been protected by his cap but the rest of his face was red and bristled with short yellow hairs. His eyes were like two bright nails behind his gold-rimmed spectacles that had been mended over the nose with haywire. His whole face looked as if it might have been patched together out of several others." Mrs. McIntyre's complicity in the death of Guizac, which is paralleled by the larger complicity of the community as a whole, dominates the third section of the story and makes the absurdity of situation so absolute that no one, except perhaps Father Flynn, can escape from it. Not only is Guizac displaced because of his transgressions upon a rigid caste system, but following his death all the farm's inhabitants become alienated from their environment. Mrs. McIntyre suddently feels that she is in "some foreign country," and as the farm disintegrates she contracts a nervous affliction that renders her virtually indigent. Shortley and Sulk leave, and old Astor refuses to work. In the end the act of displacement comes full circle: everyone is alienated from the farm and from common humanity.

In "The Displaced Person" the imagination of the author transforms an ordinary symbol into a complex tale which assaults the opposition between Christ and culture. The pace at which the world, typified by the farm, becomes unsteady and the manner in which the placid setting is disrupted by the presence of the displaced person are exceptionally handled. In a manner suggestive of Ellison's *Invisible Man* Miss O'Connor posits an individual who is unseen by humanity. Guizac's fate thus becomes an interpretation of culture; as the historical Christ, the penultimate displaced person, he becomes the protype of the grotesque protagonist, preordained to wandering, persecution, and crucifixion.

The brutal inevitability of Guizac's death receives similar orchestration in other stories by Flannery O'Connor. In *Wise Blood*, for example, Haze's frantic attempt to escape the shadow of Jesus in the first half of the novel is later countered by equally vigorous efforts toward union with Christ through asceticism and extreme penance.

As Haze figuratively moves back to Bethlehem, his half-articulated and tortured spiritual state becomes synonymous with Christ's own agonies on the road to Calvary; eventually, in a grotesque crucifixion scene, he is clubbed unconscious by two policemen and brought home dead, although his landlady continues to talk to him as though he were the resurrected Christ.

Still another Christ figure, O. E. Parker, the protagonist in the superlative story "Parker's Back" (1965), is the most engaging of Flannery O'Connor's grotesques, perhaps because he is one of the few who are not harmful or seriously harmed. When Parker has a Byzantine Christ tattooed on his back, he undergoes a remarkable transformation in which he literally becomes identified with the numerous bearers of religious mystery who serve to rejuvenate society and to form its consciousness. The Christ on Parker's back is a genuine presence: Parker himself is altered by its mystical power—a power which loses its force only when there is a shift to a rational point of view, where the mystic symbol becomes a mere sign, quite conventional and ridiculous, as it is to Parker's wife.

The reaction of Parker's wife to his tattoo is a carefully executed stroke of irony. This reception by Sarah Ruth is delightfully comic, but on a more serious level it is a prefiguration of the Crucifixion: as Parker stands before the barred door, he is shocked by the revelation of a tree of fire, and he falls backward against the door "as if he had been pinned there by a lance." It is at this moment that Parker's transformation is complete: previously possessed by Christ, he now becomes identified with Him. The story then ends in an absurd imitation of the death of Christ. Parker's "death" comes at the hands of his incensed wife, who is outraged by his latest tattoo. Any picture of God is merely an indication of idolatry to her, and she thus subjects her husband to yet another purgation, this time with a broom. She beats him until large welts appear on the face of the tattooed Christ. Parker comically emulates the passion of Christ. He does not die, however, as did his predecessors Haze Motes and Guizac, and he remains in the world. He becomes a child of Christ and, we may assume, attains a higher reality and a higher consciousness, for by taking up the Cross, he finally loses his ego.

O. E. Parker might well be the author's greatest comic grotesque. The story itself certainly is a masterpiece, tightly organized and remarkable in its pictorial quality. Miss O'Connor's regard for figure and perspective creates a memorable figure and an extraordinary situation. The story's insistence upon the ambiguities of existence, and upon the pain and suffering of life are skillfully evoked. And in its imaginative use of materials, the story is as picaresque as anything Flannery O'Connor wrote.

Parker's complaint arises not only from his own obsessions, but also from a dialectical opposition to the religious groundings of his culture. In a sense all the author's misbelievers, who range from the falsely pious to the thoroughly damned, are cultural grotesques: the enduring values of their society throw their miscreant behavior into stark focus. In her fictive world common existence is seemingly limited and provincial; but a single religion, the old backwoods Fundamentalism, still dominates, and this makes for piety and awe, as well as for madness and violence. The squalid cities and towns, the piedmont farms, the sinister topography of pine tree and sand flat, of shabby movie marquees and Jesus Saves signs, impress themselves upon the protagonists' sensibilities until the very physical and spiritual qualities of the landscape are linked with their destinies. The result of this amalgamation is almost always disorder, a chaotic mental state in the characters which is balanced only by the ordering power of Miss O'Connor's fiction.

Beneath the descriptive simplicity of these settings there is a pervasive feeling of character conditioned by a lingering social framework. Individual experience is a reflection of this milieu, and thus there is a distinct symmetry between the behavior of Flannery O'Connor's grotesques and the culture that spawned them. Although there is no counterpart in her fiction to Faulkner's Yoknapatawpha, to Eudora Welty's Natchez Trace, or to the dark and bloody ground of Robert Penn Warren, O'Connor's writing does bear an intrinsic relationship to the historicity of her region. As she observed in her essay "The Catholic Novelist in the Protestant South":

> The two circumstances that have given character to my own writing have been those of being Southern and being Catholic. This is considered by many to be an unlikely combination, but I have found it to be a most likely one. I think that the South provides the Catholic novelist with some benefits that he usually lacks, and lacks to a conspicuous degree. The Catholic novel can't be categorized by subject matter, but only by what it assumes about human and divine reality. It cannot see man as determined; it cannot see him as totally depraved. It will see him as incomplete in himself, as prone to evil, but as redeemable when his own efforts are assisted by grace. And it will see this grace as working through nature, but as entirely transcending it, so that a door is always open to possibility and the unexpected in the human soul.[11]

The operation of grace through nature is one of the author's major fictional and religious concerns, and this explains why she valued her region and its culture so highly — precisely because it revealed certain manifestations of the spirit grounded in the concrete world. This spiritual dimension of reality led Miss O'Connor to remark in "The Regional Writer": "To call yourself a Georgia writer is certainly to declare a limitation, but one which, like all limitations, is a gateway to reality. It is a great blessing, perhaps the greatest blessing a writer can have, to find at home what others have to go elsewhere seeking."[12] The South provided Miss O'Connor with two main attributes of her fiction — a sense of manners and a sense of religious mystery. Manners are a part of the concrete world which every serious novelist must acknowledge. "You get manners," she observed in "Writing Short Stories," "from the texture of existence that surrounds you. The great advantage of being a Southern writer is that we don't have to go anywhere to look for manners; bad or good, we've got them in abundance. We in the South live in a society that is rich in contradiction, rich in irony, rich in contrast, and particularly rich in speech."[13] This sense of historical ambiguity, rooted in the concrete, extends outward until it embraces the realm of mystery, and the coincidence of these two qualities, as Robert Heilman has observed in one of the most penetrating essays on the nature of southern literature, is what makes the fiction of this region so distinctive. Heilman terms the sense of mystery a "sense of totality," yet it is easy to discern that he and Miss O'Connor are discussing the same phenomenon:

> Inclined to question whether suffering is totally eliminatable or unequivocally evil, the Southerners are most aware that, as Tate has put it, man is incurably religious, and that the critical problem is not one of skeptically analyzing the religious impulse of thinking as if religion did not exist for a mature individual and culture, but of distinguishing the real thing and the surrogates. . . . For them, totality is more than the sum of the sensory and the rational. The invention of gods is a mark, not of a passion for unreality, but of a high sense of reality; is not a regrettable flight from science, but perhaps a closer approach to the problem of being.[14]

The burden which a sense of reality and of mystery imposes upon a writer is one of honesty toward one's region, rather than of slavish devotion to it. As Miss O'Connor mentioned in "The Fiction Writer and His Country," truthful depiction of these two qualities requires "a delicate adjustment of the outer and inner worlds, in such a way that, without changing their nature, they can be seen through each other. To know oneself is to know one's region. It is also to know the world, and it is also, paradoxically, a form of exile from that world."[15] To be an exile from the world implies a detachment from it, and this in turn permits a degree of objectivity in rendering it. This feeling of exile places O'Connor at the center of what Lewis Simpson, in an elegant and carefully wrought investigation of the southern writer, terms the Great Literary Secession.[16] Miss O'Connor is able to appreciate the cultural and historical richness of her region because of this detachment, which does not negate her willingness to utilize the South's firm guidelines: ". . . these guides have to exist in a concrete form, known and held sacred by the whole community. They have to exist in the form of stories which affect our image and our judgement of ourselves."[17] By being in partial exile from her region, Flannery O'Connor never succumbs to what C. Van Woodward has called those illusions of innocence and virtue which afflict all aspects of the southern mind — and the broader American character as well.

Considered from this perspective, General Tennessee Flintrock Sash, the one hundred and four year-old artifact of the Civil War in the story "A Late Encounter With the Enemy" (1953), is the epitome of the cultural grotesque, because he represents not the substance of a tradition (for he wasn't really a general in the war), but rather the dessication of it. As the representative of a dying tradition General Sash is appropriately more dead than alive: part of his body is already petrified, and the rest of him has atrophied to the point where he is "as frail as a spider." Even his name, Flintrock, is suggestive, for it implies that he is hard and inanimate. One of the finest touches in this story—his continual metamorphosis into a relic—reinforces this impression of his inanimate character. The general has been used as a Hollywood publicity gimmick, and he is loaned annually to the museum for Confederate Memorial Day; and when the antebellum homes are opened in the springtime, he is invited "to wear his uniform and sit in some conspicuous spot and lend atmosphere to the scene." This depiction is consummately humorous, permitting the story to be enjoyed as a satire on the southern myth of magnolias and moonlight—on what Stark Young, one of the perpetrators of this myth, was fond of calling the art of living. On another level, however, the comedy implicit in the story is annihilating: its destructive force is employed in such a way as to produce an estrangement within the cultural setting that is typical of the grotesque.

Both the general and his granddaughter, Sally Poker Sash, confuse the past with the present, a complicated circumstance in which the laws of causality are seemingly suspended. Their invincibility is predicated upon their ability to resuscitate the old traditions of dignity, honor, and courage; but these are effectively challenged by their own vanity and by two symbols of modernity—a Boy Scout who leaves the general sitting in the sun, thereby precipitating his stroke, and a Coca Cola machine. Thus the ultimate enemy to which the title of the story alludes is this new tradition, for the parable of historical glory is grotesquely undercut by these new cultural symbols.

In a story like "A Late Encounter With the Enemy" the author's effort to deal with the implications of time and of history reveals her as both native and alien to her region. To the extent that many of the themes in this story — death and decay, the sense of guilt, alienation and isolation, the destruction of values, the conflict between generations — have counterparts in the history of the South, it is easy to see why the regional flavor of her fiction gave Miss O'Connor what she termed a degree of advantage over less privileged writers in other parts of the United States. Yet there is a larger perspective which this history forces upon her, and which she sought to explore in all of her fiction:

When Walker Percy won the National Book Award, newsmen asked him why there were so many good Southern writers and he said, "Because we lost the War." He didn't mean by that simply that a lost war makes good subject matter. What he was saying was that we have had our Fall. We have gone into the modern world with an inburnt knowledge of human limitations and with a sense of mystery which could not have developed in our first state of innocence — as it has not sufficiently developed in the rest of the country.

Not every lost war would have this effect on every society, but we are doubly blessed, not only in our Fall, but in having the means to interpret it. Behind our own history, deepening it at every point, has been another history. Mencken called the South the Bible Belt, in scorn and thus in incredible innocence. In the South we have, in however attenuated form, a vision of Moses' face as he pulverized the idols. This knowledge is what makes the Georgia writer different from the writer of Hollywood or New York. It is the knowledge that the novelist finds in his community. When he ceases to find it there, he will cease to write, or at least he will cease to write anything enduring. The writer operates at a peculiar crossroads where time and place and eternity somehow meet. His problem is to find that location.[18]

In her facetious moments Miss O'Connor was fond of asserting that to be a Georgia author was "a rather specious dignity, on the same order as, for the pig, being a Talmadge ham."[19] Yet seen within the larger context analyzed above, it is obvious that for her the term "regional writer" was certainly a valuable restriction. Indeed her origins were an asset, because Flannery O'Connor realized that the interplay of social and religious forces in the South worked to produce both characters and situations that were inherently grotesque. Thus, when asked why she wrote about grotesque characters, she replied:

> Because we can still recognize one. In the South, where most people still believe in original sin, our sense of evil is still just strong enough to make us skeptical about most modern solutions, no matter how long we embrace them. We are still held by a sense of mystery, however much against our will. The prophet-freaks of Southern literature are not images of the man in the street. They are images of man forced out to meet the extremes of his own nature. The writer owes a great debt to everything he sees around him, and in Georgia he is particularly blessed in having about him a collection of goods and evils which are intensely stimulating to the imagination.[20]

Realizing that the South was "Christ-haunted and that ghosts cast strange shadows, very fierce shadows, particularly in our literature,"[21] Miss O'Connor made the vast majority of her characters attest to a religious presence by either fanatically embracing or denying it, by remaining dangerously apathetic about it, or by replacing it with a more contemporary explanation of human destiny. The communal displacement which is so evident in her "farm" stories, for example, serves as an index of the spiritual displacement of the characters. With a regional background rooted in a sense of evil and of original sin, incredible grotesques emerge, since the history of the area tends to foster extreme behavior.

Delineation of the cultural grotesque as a main char-

acter type establishes Flannery O'Connor as a very
special kind of regionalist, as one who both utilizes the
South's special resources and who is decidedly at odds
with it, for what she once described as the division of
Christendom is rooted largely in the failure of community. Her cultural grotesques do not cultivate the land
but instead pursue moral and spiritual decay. They debase their own traditions, and consequently Miss O'Connor found little civic virtue in her rural folk. She assailed
the myth of agrarian perfection promulgated from Jef-
ferson to Allen Tate. This led her to conclude that the
Catholic novelist in the Protestant South "will feel a good
deal more kinship with backwoods prophets and shouting fundamentalists than he will with those politer elements for whom the supernatural is an embarrassment
and for whom religion has become a department of
sociology or culture or personality development."[22]
Realizing that the Agrarians could no longer speak for
her generation, she evolved a new attitude based on
physical and spiritual isolation within the community.
Her fiction reveals that the norms of southern life have
lost their sacredness and have become disastrously secular in orientation. The reality of this situation in turn
forced her to concentrate upon the atypicality of southern
life, because the new southern identity must derive not
"from the mean average or the typical, but from the hidden and often the most extreme."[23]

For Flannery O'Connor communal life in the South
should have a spiritual basis, yet its very absence forced
her not only to attack this dissociation but also to locate
the divine in the extreme. "I am always having it pointed
out to me," she wrote, "that life in Georgia is not at all
the way I picture it, that escaped criminals do not roam
the roads exterminating families, nor Bible salesmen
prowl about looking for girls with wooden legs."[24] The

point is that people like the Misfit and the Bible salesman, or the insane Singleton of the uncollected story
"The Partridge Festival" (1961), who kills even more
people than the Misfit, are necessary in order to force a
recognition of man's radical dependence on God upon
the average man. The true cultural grotesques are the invariably well-mannered members of the community who
ignore the spiritual foundations of their culture. Miss
O'Connor sees the South as struggling to preserve this
spiritual identity, not only against the Raybers and the
Sheppards, but also against those numerous members
of the community who substitute sanctimoniousness for
true Christian virtue. This insight into human nature
applies especially well to her earth mothers—to Mrs.
May in "Greenleaf," to Mrs. McIntyre in "The Displaced Person," to Mrs. Cope in "A Circle in the Fire,"
and to Mrs. Turpin in "Revelation." These women traipse
their fields, pastures, and woods with a singleminded
sense of righteous proprietorship that prevents them from
recognizing a fundamentally spiritual estrangement from
their surroundings, an estrangement rooted in their in-
ability to act charitably toward their neighbors. Unaware
of their alienation, these ordinary individuals are extremely vulnerable to extraordinary events which test
their harshness and rigidity of spirit.

One of the most remarkable of these cultural grotesques is Ruby Turpin, the protagonist of Flannery
O'Connor's short story, "Revelation." Unlike many writers whose energies atrophy in middle age, Miss O'Connor
had talents that were constantly improving, and a story
as nearly flawless as "Revelation" (which won a post-
humous first prize in the O'Henry competitions) is a
poignant testament to a talent thwarted by death. First
published in the *Sewanee Review* in 1964, it is a fable of
God's providence operating in a doctor's office and in a

pig pen. A triumph of the comic grotesque, the story opens in a doctor's waiting room, where an extraordinary collection of patients who form a miniature society—a ship of fools—awaits examination. Assembled in this almost claustrophobic office are representative diseases of the body, the mind, and the spirit: the crippled bodies of the aged, the maimed intelligences of the poor and the neuroses of the intellectually gifted, and the defective souls of the self-righteous. Their illnesses represent the maladies of society, and the traits of this society are progressively revealed to a point where the absurdity implicit in the characters' behavior must explode.

Ruby Turpin, who self-indulgently speculates about the blessings bestowed on her by the Lord, unconsciously turns the story into a punitive fable on arrogance, hypocrisy, and pride. She gradually emerges as a high-toned Christian lady whose sense of social and moral superiority and whose extreme self-absorption and pride border on narcissism. Negative aspects of her character are progressively revealed and thrown into grotesque perspective, and each brushstroke fills in a canvas that is unrelieved by any redeeming qualities. Mindless of her faults, she establishes herself as a type of white culture heroine, aligned with a pitiful minority against the encroachments of Negroes, poor-white trash, and the baser elements of humanity. Because of her obsessions and her spiritual deformities she is inherently grotesque; her thoughts and her actions reveal her as a negative moral agent, unaware of her own absurdity because she is so attached to an inauthentic existence.

It is relevant that Miss O'Connor plots this story at a pace that is discernibly slower than most of her short fiction and that Ruby's unbearable self-righteousness is gradually reinforced to the point of the reader's exasperation. The lack of any physical action, counterpointed by

Ruby's constant speculation on the mysteries of creation and by the mechanical conversation of the patients, creates a repressed narrative pace wherein the slightest disruption in movement could have the unusual effect of releasing tensions which lie just beneath the surface of the story. Thus the dramatic escalation which occurs abruptly after Ruby thanks the Lord for having created in her such a fine creature is so unanticipated that the shocking impact creates one of the revelations to which the title of the story alludes. As the Wellesley girl strikes Ruby Turpin in the eye with a hurled book and pounces on her in a frenzy, the astonishing disclosure of the girl's imprecation is not only authoritative in moral terms, but approximates, as perfectly as the literary medium can, the actual force of revelation.

The execration which the girl hurls at Ruby Turpin is both shocking and convincing, for it calls Ruby's self-contained egocentric existence into question. Ruby tries to rebel against this revelation, which in theological terms is a manifestation of God's providence, and which in emotional terms is cathartic. Because of this revelation she becomes an inhabitant of a world which suddenly appears estranged to her. Her initial revelation – that she is, in the girl's words, a wart-hog from hell – is at first incomprehensible and then outrageous, and the remainder of the story traces the process whereby she painfully learns obedience, which is a prerequisite of true faith and of salvation.

Ruby's failure to present a suitable defense of herself shifts from outrage to hatred and bitterness toward God, and the image of this woman marching out to the pig parlour to wage battle with the Lord is a brilliant and hilarious picture of the false believer journeying to meet her apocalypse. Still actively engaged in an attempt to reconstruct the world in her own image, she subsumes any conception of God to her own blueprint, an act that constitutes absolute heresy. This is her central crisis — and the crisis of all of Flannery O'Connor's cultural grotesques: as the landscape transforms itself from the brightness of late afternoon to a deepening and mysterious blue, the reality of this crisis begins to catch up with her.

Ruby Turpin is one of the author's countless grotesques who are largely the creations of themselves. Their own misconception of self and of social laws places them in opposition to a higher justice which assures the ultimate triumph of their opposites — the humble and the meek. Assuredly the lame shall enter first, while the superior citizen, conducting his life for his own sake, shall suffer a humiliation even more acute than total damnation.

Conscious elaboration of the cultural grotesque was merely a part of Flannery O'Connor's incisive depiction of degeneracy at all social levels. All her characters are susceptible to defects in nature and spirit, and these deficiencies are what estrange them from the community and from God. Whether it is Haze Motes trying nihilistically to overturn his culture, or Ruby Turpin attempting to preserve it, Miss O'Connor ridicules pride and hypocrisy wherever she finds it. She unmasks her grotesques by exposing their perversity, affectation, and vanity, and she frequently reduces them to impotence through satire. For O'Connor it is the grotesque which underlies all forms of failure. Revealing the dilemmas in the quest for human identity, she shows how the lack of an integrated society — which for the author would be a Christian society — prevents the possibility of an integrated personality. All her grotesques eventually come to the realization of the fact that they are aspiring toward illusory points in a secular world. This defect in vision, epitomized by Haze Motes, whose very name suggests his confused condition, creates an abnormality which is not easily cured.

The grotesques of Flannery O'Connor are individuals who cannot erase the horrors of their obsessions. Few images of peace and beauty populate their world, few are the interludes of order. Implicit in their behavior are all the conventions of the grotesque—the nightmare world, the perversion, the satanic humor. These people wear their deficiencies of spirit as scars—as emblems of a world without order, meaning, or sense of continuity. In an attempt to transcend their painful condition, to rise above that which is alienated and estranged, Miss O'Connor's protagonists invariably descend into the demonic. Obsessed with their own sins, with weakness, evil, and suffering, they turn inward upon themselves and act out their agonies in extraordinary ways. Because O'Connor's grotesques are—to paraphrase T. S. Eliot in his essay on Baudelaire—men enough to be saved or damned, their actions in this world become reflections of the interior life of the soul. It is one of the triumphs of Flannery O'Connor's art—and a mark of her vital faith—that she is willing to write about all types of malefactors who, utterly out of harmony with the world and with Creation, risk exile and damnation for their disbelief.

Grotesque Action

The Metaphor of Journey

Chapter Three In giving over much of her creative energy to the development of such memorable grotesques as the Misfit and the Bible salesman, Flannery O'Connor realized that her method of character depiction could be successful only to the extent that her protagonists were involved in significant action, in varieties of plot which served to illuminate the nature of the problems which these protagonists confronted. She accepted as axiomatic the assumption that character exists only in action, that only action produces and formulates characters and dramatizes major issues. Certainly this coincidence of character, action, and idea must have impressed Miss O'Connor as she read the work of one of her favorite authors, Henry James, who in his later novels evolved a theory of the moral and dramatic sense which resembles her own fictional strategy.

More often than not O'Connor formulates grotesque characterization through a definite pattern of action designed to create and to enlarge clear lines of conflict. This variety of action, which is as old as the *Odyssey,* is the narrative of quest, a type which embraces such seemingly disparate forms as epic, allegory, the picaresque novel, and much of the grotesque. Charles Walcutt, in his incisive study of the varieties of characterization and action in literature, suggests how pervasive this theme of quest is:

Conrad's "Heart of Darkness," Melville's *Moby Dick*, Hawthorne's "Young Goodman Brown," Mark Twain's *Huckle-
berry Finn*, and Katherine Anne Porter's *Ship of Fools* use
the journey as at once a form and a symbol.... Their journeys penetrate into darker and darker regions which cor-
respond to states of mind and conditions of man. The voyager
makes a journey into his own spirit as he penetrates the
human conditions that are both physically and symbolically
presented. Observation and discovery, although enacted
apart from the typical social setting, become social, psychological, and even philosophical.[1]

Walcutt's allusion to journey as form and symbol is illuminating: the narrative of quest provides on the one
hand clearly delineated stages of action through which
the protagonist passes and on the other hand an image of
man who is forced to confront the ambiguities of existence. This literature of quest therefore frequently constitutes a narrative of extremes, wherein the possibilities
of salvation and damnation, escape and entrapment,
chaos and order exist in radical tension. Like Bunyan's
Christian the typical protagonist embarks on a journey
which in reality is a contest, a heightened exercise in
consciousness, perception, and endurance whereby man
is either conquered or triumphant in his battle with the
forces of darkness.

Obviously the literature of quest was congenial to Miss
O'Connor's imagination. She understood the manifold
possibilities of quest as reflections of grotesque action —
as narrative which estranges man from his physical and
metaphysical universe, but which paradoxically offers
man the prospect of regeneration and reintegration if the
horrors of the metaphorical quest are successfully overcome. One of her treasured quotations, from St. Cyril of
Jerusalem, suggests the possibilities of grotesque action
that are inherent in the dark voyage:

> "The dragon sits by the side of the road, watching those who
> pass. Beware lest he devour you. We go to the Father of
> Souls, but it is necessary to pass by the Dragon." No matter
> what form the dragon may take, it is of this mysterious pas-
> sage past him, or into his jaws, that stories of any depth will
> always be concerned to tell, and this being the case, it
> requires considerable courage at any time, in any country,
> not to turn away from the storyteller.[2]

Confrontation with the dragon, who assumes many guises
in grotesque literature that utilizes the metaphor of
journey, is the entire purpose of the quest. It is the dragon
who personifies the discontinuities and destructive force
of the absurd world and who makes the grotesque protagonist's rage for order that much more acute. Understood in this light, it is easy to see why much modern
literature of the grotesque is so susceptible to metaphors
of voyage; novels like *Ulysses, The Castle, Lolita, As I
Lay Dying,* and *The Tin Drum,* which are purely or par-
tially grotesque in vision and technique, reveal that the
rite de passage is perhaps the typical variety of action
that we encounter in absurd fiction.

Many of Flannery O'Connor's protagonists are engaged
in psychological and spiritual quests, and the physical
voyages which they undertake serve to locate the meaning of the story and to provide a structure for it. The protagonists in her first story, "The Geranium," and its
sequel, "Judgment Day," are obsessed with imaginary
journeys home; the antiheroes in Miss O'Connor's two
novels are in impossible pursuit of a world without Christ;
the absurd family trip in "A Good Man is Hard to Find"
devolves into a violent encounter with destiny and the
forces of evil; the young boy in "The River" embarks on
a trip that is shrouded in theological mystery and which
provokes ambivalent responses to the conclusion; Head

and Nelson in "The Artificial Nigger" make a pilgrimage into a Dantesque hell in order to receive grace; Tom T. Shiftlet forsakes his soul for a motor car that shall provide his justification and his means of travel; the young girl in "A Temple of the Holy Ghost" makes a seemingly harmless excursion to a carnival that harbors a curious presence; Asbury in "The Enduring Chill" journeys home to die, only to encounter forces that are stronger than his impulse toward destruction; the bus trip which Julian takes with his mother in "Everything That Rises Must Converge" ends in death and total disorientation; the inimitable O. E. Parker constructs his own road to Calvary; the boy and girl in "The Partridge Festival" make a pedagogical journey to the state insane asylum to see an individual whom they variously consider as Everyman and Christ. Thus, in both of O'Connor's novels and more than half of her short stories, episodes of quest serve as penultimate examples of life enacted as an ordeal, as descents into the dark night of the soul, where dragons and other fierce monsters, frequently in human form, await their unsuspecting victims.

Quest, then, is the basic metaphor of action in Flannery O'Connor's fiction. It is the spirit that animates her work and that permits her to concentrate upon extremes of behavior and to explore ultimate things. Her fiction gives the impression that in the enactment of the quest experience, all action becomes symbolic, as in the fiction of Hawthorne and Kafka. Through the quest motif, Miss O'Connor can maneuver her characters into sharply defined situations which force them to confront that religious mystery which the author sees at the center of experience — that felt presence which can never be wholly understood, which exists but is inexplicable. As a Catholic, who insisted on the moral sense in literature and who realized that to render it successfully an inordinate amount of drama was necessary, she made ingenious efforts to produce narratives involving heightened actions, where events exist to make ideas and characters comprehensible. This sort of technical strategy is easily identifiable in her fiction: events are magnified and culminate in murder, theft, hanging, blinding, drowning, and conflagration; deceptions, madness, and schizophrenia force a rapid narrative pace; visions of mayhem and chaos become centers of dramatic and moral interest, thus instilling the quest motif with a grotesque ambience.

The paths which Miss O'Connor's protagonists take are not frivolous, although they are permeated with a brand of demonic humor. Generally speaking, these quests are ascetic, and the voyage itself is mystical, a fact which defines an important aspect of O'Connor's imagination, for she interpreted existence as a mystical phenomenon. There are, as Evelyn Underhill pointed out in her classic study of mysticism, various stages in the mystical way. These include the awakening of the self, the purification of self, illumination, the dark night of the soul, and union.[3] Miss Underhill admits that this classification is somewhat arbitrary and that stages tend to merge or reverse themselves. Nevertheless, all these stages can be detected in O'Connor's fiction, although the overall pattern, except in perfect allegories like "The Artificial Nigger," is never as rigid as Underhill's framework suggests. However, although the paths which Flannery O'Connor's characters take are obscure and even unknown, invariably they lead to confrontations with God or with Satan. Quite frequently the protagonists are deprived of ultimate mystical union; but the voyagers, whether they are saved or damned, are subjected to terrifying events, which are necessary if they are to be purged. Indeed there is little in Miss O'Connor's fiction that ameliorates the dreadfulness of her characters' forced voyages beneath the shadow of the dragon. Destruction, either physical or spiritual, awaits many of them, and the precious few who emerge at the end of their journey are transformed by their confrontations with evil or with mystery.

Action conceived as a quest into the mysteries of existence produces a narrative which frequently is revelatory for Miss O'Connor's characters. Once they awaken to the alternatives which confront them, their decisions become crucial to their own physical and spiritual wellbeing; the degree of human growth or development of consciousness which they are capable of depends upon how they respond to a series of incidents which are inherently dangerous and potentially absurd. In other words grotesque action forces characters to evaluate their conduct. This is true even of the children, who possess the curiously developed, if not refined, intelligences which we immediately associate with such child-heroes in American fiction as Huck Finn and Holden Caulfield. What is astonishing about Flannery O'Connor's children is that they usually manage to interpret moral and spiritual phenomena correctly, whereas their adult superiors continually distort the significance of events. This division between the purity of the child's vision and the diseased intellect of the adult is apparent in a number of Miss O'Connor's stories, including "The Artificial Nigger," "The River," "A Temple of the Holy Ghost," and "The Lame Shall Enter First."

From the tenor of her fiction it seems evident that Flannery O'Connor thought that the child was capable of perceiving moral and spiritual chaos better than the adult, because his experience is never exclusively intellectual. In a letter to Ihab Hassan she notes that children see nothing unusual in the grotesque and tend to accept it as a view of reality. "When a child draws," she writes, "he doesn't try to be grotesque but to set down exactly what he sees, and as his gaze is direct, he sees the lines that create motion."[4] What Miss O'Connor apparently is emphasizing is that children do not recognize categories that limit vision. A child sees and accepts distortion, the fusion of animate and inanimate, the mingling of dream and reality, and horror relieved by laughter; this is the child's vision, and the discrepancy between his view of reality and that conceived by the adult world contributes to a grotesque effect. O'Connor's children accept the grotesque because it is predicated upon ambiguity and contradiction; they accept as axiomatic the incongruous nature of reality. They reject categories because they are simplifications of reality.

The child voyager thus is confronted with action in a world which does not admit to placid ordering. He is redeemed from the beginning because he apprehends the lines which create spiritual motion. Yet his journey is an initiation into a world which for him is fascinating and puzzling. Consequently the action in a story like "The River" (1954), moves away from the security and bland order of the community into a world where all activity is presented as a test of courage and commitment. This story, from Miss O'Connor's first collection, particularly reveals how a liturgical spirit—that is to say, how the process whereby an individual becomes aware of logos, of Christ and the world—informs the destiny of the child who is involved in grotesque action. Young Harry Ashfield in "The River" is a child who suffers emotional and spiritual privation in an alcoholic and atheistic family. He is initiated into the context of Christianity by his babysitter, who shows him a book entitled "The Life of Jesus Christ for Readers Under Twelve" and who takes him to a faith-healing at the river. After he is baptized by the preacher in the river, Harry is told that he is now a member of the Elect. But his parents mock their son's spiritual encounter. The next morning Harry returns to the river, which he now associates with the River of Life, and forces himself beneath its surface, thus beginning his journey toward a more promising country.

Faith to a rational individual is a matter of intelligence and will, but the crisis of faith which Harry Ashfield experiences is obsessional and represents a passage through the dark night of the soul. This passage is revealed by a consistent pattern of imagery, and through a complicated relationship between the boy and the preacher, in which a complete presentation of the possibilities of faith or denial are worked out. Early in the story two motifs begin to develop which are crucial to the resolution. First, as soon as the boy learns that the preacher's name is Bevel Summers, he appropriates the forename and convinces his new babysitter of the remarkable coincidence. Second, as he is playing with the babysitter's children, Harry-Bevel is tempted to remove a board in the pig pen; an enraged shoat attacks him, roots him to the ground, and chases him in a panic to the house.

The second episode, in which Harry-Bevel is terrified by the shoat, provides the main recurring image in the story. When Mrs. Connin reads to him from the book about Jesus, he encounters a picture which he finds unusually impressive: "It was full of pictures, one of the carpenter driving a crowd of pigs out of a man. They were real pigs, gray and sour-looking, and Mrs. Connin said Jesus had driven them all out of this one man." The original shoat was "longlegged and humpbacked and part of one of his ears had been bitten off"; it reminds Mrs. Connin of a certain Mr. Paradise, who has a cancerous deformity on his ear. Thus, when Harry-Bevel encounters Mr. Paradise at the faith healing, he is terrified by the old man, whose grotesque appearance reminds him of the shoat. Mr. Paradise, as I have noted, is the incarnation of the devil. As a confirmed disbeliever he symbolizes all forces of evil; he stands in opposition to the young preacher, whom he ridicules. His name is ironical, because he offers a false paradise. The significance of the bulge on his temple is not overlooked by the preacher, who cries, " 'Believe Jesus or the Devil!' "

At the conclusion of the story Mr. Paradise follows the boy to the river, carrying with him an enormous peppermint stick with which he plans to seduce the child. Ironically he propels Harry-Bevel away from the world of evil toward his ultimate destination; when the boy, already standing in the river turns toward the shore, he sees "something like a giant pig bounding after him, shaking a red and white club and shouting." The boy submerges in fright, and as he drifts toward unconsciousness and death, the old anxieties disappear; he is now on his way to the perfect kingdom, for the Tempter of Souls has been overcome.

It is evident that the swine imagery—connecting the live shoat, the illustration of Jesus harrowing pigs from a man, and the demonic figure of Mr. Paradise—is designed to establish the forces of evil and disbelief which Harry-Bevel encounters during his quest. Juxtaposed against these sinister forces is a set of more obvious ancillary relationships: the boy's literal identification with the evangelist and his increasing awareness of Christ which culminates in a literal acceptance of His kingdom. Because he has been baptized, Harry partakes of Christ by identifying himself with the preacher, who is a surrogate of Christ, and by immersing himself in the blood-red river, which is the River of Life. Thus the climax of Harry's journey reveals that to rise above the alienated and the estranged requires a transcending leap of faith. All the action preceding this climax elucidates the process whereby human beings, estranged from the common world and perplexed by the unknown, penetrate a larger world in order to leave the absurd one behind. Harry Ashfield, confronting a meaningless and terrifying void in his daily circumstance, must test himself at every stage in his journey; eventually he manages to emerge from his conflict with the dragon into a finer spiritual insight, but even this ultimate perception is shrouded in ambiguity.

The child protagonists in Miss O'Connor's fiction do not always understand the workings of grace, but somehow they manage to penetrate it at the end of their journeys, perhaps because they learn to accept the interrelation of the temporal and the spiritual. This is true of Norton in "The Lame Shall Enter First" who like Harry Ashfield embarks on a rather startling voyage in search of a heavenly guardian, of Nelson in "The Artificial Nigger" who senses the presence of grace in a suffering statue, and of the young girl in "A Temple of the Holy Ghost" who is initiated into the ravages of sin and suffering through the mysteries of sex and of the consecrated Host. What characterizes these child initiates is the fact that at the beginning of their quests they are entirely divorced from any spiritual experience and that their lives are fragmented and dissociated. Their alienation is caused by an opposition between the temporal and the eternal, and Miss O'Connor moves them through stages of a mystical quest in order to reveal the possibilities of synthesizing the secular and the holy. Grotesque action, conceived of as a metaphor of journey, thus guides these children in the apprehension of God.

To be certain, Flannery O'Connor's children are capable of fierce rebellion, but this rebellion merely accentuates the need of saving grace. This observation best applies to *The Violent Bear It Away*, where the metaphor

of quest is embodied in young Tarwater's search for a
vocation. Miss O'Connor spent eight years in writing
this novel, and the theme which emerges from the tight
triangular conflict between Tarwater, his great-uncle, and
his uncle is perfectly delineated. As the author remarked:
"I wanted to get across the fact that the great-uncle (old
Tarwater) is the Christian—a sort of crypto-Catholic—
and that the schoolteacher (Rayber) is the typical modern
man. The boy (young Tarwater) has to choose which one,
which way, he wants to follow. It is a matter of vocation."[5]
Thus throughout the novel Francis Marion Tarwater is
doubly alienated: first from the fanaticism of his great-
uncle, a prophet who had lived in the world for other-
worldly ends; and from his uncle, a militant atheist who
lives in and for the world.

Grotesque action, centered upon Tarwater's quest for
a vocation, is sharply scenic in this novel, and invariably
terse and ironic; most noticeable is its rapidity, induced
by an emphasis upon violence, mayhem, shock, and the
unexpected. These fictional strategies, which are apparent in most of O'Connor's fiction, permit the author
to narrate an exciting tale, for more than once she
intimated that the story itself is fiction's best defense of
its existence; for her, a good story "would be one which
continues to rattle on at a great rate at the same time it
reaches a profound level of meaning."[6] Faithful to her
own stricture, Miss O'Connor conceived of stories which
depend on grotesque action to engender levels of meaning that offer insights into observed reality, into the
seemingly obscure motivations of men, and into such
moral and theological problems as the nature of good and
evil, the origin of sin, the reality of temptation, and the
burden of free will—to mention some of the concerns
illuminated by the narrative method of *The Violent Bear
It Away.*

The novel opens with a carefully detailed sentence that ironically undercuts young Tarwater's subsequent attempts to renounce the vocation that is seemingly preordained for him:

> Francis Marion Tarwater's uncle had been dead for only half a day when the boy got too drunk to finish digging his grave and a Negro named Buford Munson, who had come to get a jug filled, had to finish it and drag the body from the breakfast table where it was still sitting and bury it in a decent Christian way, with the sign of its Saviour at the head of the grave and enough dirt on top to keep the dogs from digging it up.

Here, and throughout the novel, authorial omniscience is refined to the point where it becomes a private joke involving the writer and the reader, because the first sentence provides information which Tarwater never knows until the end of his quest. Tarwater, after he returns from the still, sets the shack on fire, thinking that his great-uncle's corpse is still inside. The "immense silver eyes" which he envisions in the flames are those of the outraged old man, who had entrusted the boy with two obligations which he intends to renounce: to provide old Tarwater with a decent Christian burial and to baptize Rayber's dim-witted child, Bishop. All Tarwater's subsequent actions are based on the assumption that he can enact a complete renunciation of the old man.

Like most of Miss O'Connor's grotesques young Tarwater is trapped by circumstances and by his own futile actions. The narrative, like Tarwater's quest, becomes a hazardous road which the protagonist is compelled to travel:

> The story always had to be taken to completion. It was like a road that the boy had travelled on so often that half the time

> he didn't look where they were going, and when at certain
> points he would become aware where they were, he would
> be surprised to see that the old man had not got farther on
> with it. Sometimes his uncle would lag at one point as if he
> didn't want to face what was coming and then when he
> finally came to it, he would try to get past it in a rush.

Old Tarwater persistently retells the intertwined his-
tories of Tarwater, Rayber, and himself until a rich ara-
besque forms from the story of three generations.
Underlying this story is the prophetic quest, for the narrative, convoluted and fugue-like, works inexorably
forward toward the center of mystery, which is Bishop
himself, a child blessed in his idiocy and sacramental as
Stanley Edgar Hyman in his monograph on Flannery
O'Connor astutely observed. The story shifts constantly
upon differing aspects of itself, until Tarwater considers
himself caught in a hereditary trap. To the extent that the
narrative leads always back into itself, Tarwater's efforts
to escape the burden of his mission are absurd; for him
the problem gradually becomes a need to erect faith out
of despair and hereditary guilt.

Tarwater's renunciation of his great-uncle is, of course,
ambiguous because the old man had raised the boy to be
a prophet like himself, and therefore the boy's actions
and very identity are defined by their relation to traditional belief. But assisting the boy in his renunciation is
his stranger-friend, who is one of the most foreboding
and electrifying devils in contemporary literature. It is
the stranger's voice which guides Tarwater's renunciation at every stage in his journey. By turns he reveals
himself in several avatars: he is Meeks, the copper-flue
salesman, an apostle of free enterprise whose preachings
effectively exclude any truths about the spirit; he is the
malevolent old man whom Tarwater encounters in the
park following an incident in which he almost baptizes

Bishop; and he is the pale young driver in the panama hat who drugs and sexually violates Tarwater, thereby paradoxically turning the boy back toward his prophetic mission.

It is this mission, tinged always with obsession and nightmare, which frames the grotesque action in the novel. Bishop—the object of the mission—is tangible proof of that nameless silence which continually impinges on Tarwater's free will, and he is the one object who reaffirms the mystery of existence for the boy. Old Tarwater was amazed by the Lord's wisdom in creating Bishop dim-witted so as to protect him from the corruption of Rayber, and he transfers his obsession with this unspeakable mystery to Tarwater by charging him with the duty of baptizing Bishop and thereby preserving him for Christ's legions. Tarwater, attempting to abjure his mission, reacts to Bishop with the blind fury of renunciation of a thing which is impossible to renounce. Trying to exert his free will and to avoid his apostolic destiny, he adopts a philosophy of violent and impulsive action designed to assert independence from his silent adversary. Tarwater's willful and capricious acts are grotesque because they place him in tense opposition to grace, which is a power constantly working through nature but not controlling it, since Tarwater's salvation is never certain. He is free to work out his own destiny, a point which Miss O'Connor stressed in one of her essays:

I don't think any genuine novelist is interested in writing about a world of people who are strictly determined. Even if he writes about characters who are mostly unfree, it is the sudden free action, the open possibility, which he knows is the only thing capable of illuminating the picture and giving it life. So that while predictable determined actions have a comic interest for me, it is the free act, the acceptance of grace particularly, that I always have my eye on as the thing

> which will make the story work. . . . Tarwater is certainly
> free and meant to be; if he appears to have a compulsion to
> be a prophet, I can only insist that in this compulsion there
> is the mystery of God's will for him and that it is not a com-
> pulsion in the clinical sense.[7]

Acceptance or rejection of grace and of the prophetic quest are the alternatives presented to Tarwater, and to the extent that his impulses oscillate wildly between these polarities all his action is ambivalent and incongruous. But Tarwater's quest permits a solution, for eventually he accepts the burden of his apostolic mission, which partakes of a tradition traceable to John the Baptist. It is significant that John the Baptist was a fanatic, a man who came out of the wilderness to preach the imminence of the Apocalypse and the necessity of repentance. "John the Baptist," runs a standard commentary, "actually belonged to the old order. His rite was a baptism of repentance for the remission of sins in preparation for the final judgment and the dawn of a new age."[8] His was — like Tarwater's when he turns back at the end of the novel to the city where God's children await redemption — essentially a social mission, undertaken to prepare the repentant for the fiery wrath of the Creator by washing away their sins in the River Jordan. Both Tarwaters reenact the broad configurations of John's mission. Old Mason Tarwater, like John, was a type of violent protagonist; literally forged by the fiery finger of the Lord, he transfers the messianic impulse to his great nephew who, again like John the Baptist, is driven from loneliness and isolation to faith. Because of his unpleasant experience of the city's turpitude old Tarwater has renounced his apostolic mission and returned to the wilderness, where he dies after violent wrestlings with the Lord. But the journey which Tarwater embarks upon following his great-uncle's death leads him back to the city. He too is initially defeated and returns to the wilderness, but only to emerge again at the end of the novel purified and possessed of a new spiritual and social mission that forces him back to the city.

Old Tarwater had instructed his great-nephew in rebirth and redemption and in the history of the prophets precisely so that he could know Christ; and although the boy is emotionally opposed to his prophetic mission, nothing better illustrates the way in which man adapts himself to divine knowledge than Tarwater's heresies of action and of spirit. Like his predecessor, Haze Motes, young Tarwater attempts to transform spiritual quest into blasphemy. Gradually, however, he undergoes a series of private apocalypses in which the excrescences of disbelief are blasted by wild and incomprehensible events. Tarwater is continually suffering a crisis in faith, because all of his physical acts, as well as his internal conflicts, derive from his futile attempt to remove spiritual reality from temporal dilemmas. This fragmentation of the world makes all action grotesque, and only at the conclusion of the novel does Tarwater, by receiving a direct command from God, recognize the need to force the heavenly city upon the secular city. Yet this acceptance of his mission does not simplify existence for him; he is now condemned to be a wanderer, in the great tradition of prophets who never were defeated by the recalcitrance of the secular city to repent.

Francis Marion Tarwater, of all O'Connor's protagonists who suffer similar events, stands at the center of the apostolic mission. A reluctant Jeremiah, his actions affirm the contradictory, terrifying, and violent aspects of experience which must be overcome before a person can commit himself to a vocation. His immediate difficulties create a narrative that is at once serious and totally dramatic. Tarwater serves as an image of the Christian who, retreating in the face of shifting pressures, is forced to recognize that all action is ambiguous and ultimately grotesque. His attempt to escape the burden of quest results in the same sort of ironic recognition which came to Haze Motes, Asbury, Parker, Ruby Turpin, and others.

This recognition exists even for those demonic characters who turn the metaphor of quest into a nightmare for their victims. The Misfit, despite his debased spirit and insane intelligence, understands well enough that he is seeking meaning in a world deprived of Christ; and Manly Pointer seemingly charges himself with the task of making Miss O'Connor's good country people perceive the reality of evil. Even Tom T. Shiftlet, in trying to supply himself with a usable myth, assumes the enormous burden imposed by all quests. As he says at one point to Mrs. Crater, " 'Lady, a man is divided into two parts, body and spirit. . . . A body and a spirit. . . . The body, lady, is like a house: it don't go anywhere; but the spirit, lady, is like a automobile: always on the move.' " The automobile, which is at the center of Shiftlet's body-spirit dichotomy, reveals his curiously debased logic. In a sense it is correct that the spirit wanders, but movement of the spirit should be toward God and salvation; ironically, however, Shiftlet's true movement is toward destruction and potential damnation. Shiftlet is really concerned with the body, as personfied by the automobile, which he worships and utilizes to undertake his demonic mission. Despite his proselytizing he allows himself to serve the Master of the Material by paying homage to Henry Ford. Therefore his actions are inverted, and his figuration of Christ is decadent.

Shiftlet, racing the shower to Mobile, is one of many protagonists in Flannery O'Connor's fiction who misconstrue the nature of their quest and who consequently debase it. Whereas they should be moving toward salvation, their final illumination is not one that partakes of mystical ecstasy, but rather of the tragic realization that they remain without any saving grace. In *Wise Blood*, for example, Enoch Emory's quest, providing a counterpart to Haze's, is framed by this variant of the quest motif. Enoch's "wise blood" is the impetus which makes his life a constant road to Calvary. Every day he enacts a ritual involving a trip to the park swimming pool, to the Frosty Bottle, where he drinks milkshakes and makes suggestive remarks to the waitress, to the zoo, and finally to the museum, where the Christ-mummy is housed. As he moves through these stations of the cross his wise blood guides him toward a frightening center of mystery which always eludes him at the last moment. *Wise Blood* presents us with two memorable characters — one the apotheosis of the Christian seeking his own salvation and finding it, the other a grotesque double who hounds him, exulting in its wise blood, a vivid image of man diseased in mind, deprived of grace, and seduced by the absurdity of his quest.

The absence of grace constitutes a dénouement in many of Miss O'Connor's narratives of quest, and when grace is missing the quest of necessity must remain absurd, but not without meaning. The journey of the bookish Mary Elizabeth and the cynical Calhoun to the state hospital in "The Partridge Festival" (1961) certainly disorients them, but they emerge with an image of each other as plain people, undistinguished and ungifted, who will never escape the countless azalea festivals of the future. There is no solution to Ruby Hill's dilemma in "A Stroke of Good Fortune" (1953), despite the perilous journey she undertakes up a flight of stairs; yet at the end she perceives the terror of her own inner world. Here, and in the author's more substantial fiction, the metaphor of quest is almost iconographic, in that it determines characters' reactions and the meaning of the stories. Quest transforms reality and permits a writer like Flannery O'Connor to investigate metaphysical possibilities. It places an emphasis upon shifting mirrors of perception and forces characters to revaluate their position in the world.

When characters resist the need to revaluate their own preconceptions, the world frequently disintegrates before their eyes, as it does in one of Miss O'Connor's more interesting stories, "Everything That Rises Must Converge" (1961), which takes its title from her close reading of Teilhard de Chardin. In this story a bus trip taken by Julian, a false liberal, and his racist mother serves as the metaphor of journey which results in death and disorientation. Julian, an effete college graduate who considers himself victimized by a mother who lives in a world of imaginary antebellum constructions, is obliged to accompany her every Wednesday evening to a reducing class, since she refuses to ride on integrated buses by herself. Julian, critical of others, is not aware of his own capacity for evil, and as he embarks on his journey it becomes his burden to discover his own limitations and defects. When an immense Negress and her child board the bus, Julian is exasperated by the polite games which his mother plays with the little boy, and despite his frantic protestations she insists on giving the child a shiny new penny after they get off. The Negress, infuriated by such "tokenism," attacks Julian's mother with a pocketbook, precipitating a stroke. Julian, shaken by the possibility of loss and by the depth of his own denial, is suddenly confronted with a world that is empty and incomprehensible.

This story is far more complicated than mere paraphrase indicates. To understand the nature of the quest motif in "Everything That Rises Must Converge," one has to be aware of a special variety of theological movement operative in the narrative. In *The Phenomenon of Man* Teilhard de Chardin posits a world in motion—a world basically orthogenetic which through profusion, ingenuity, and other aggregates of growth is moving from diversity toward an ultimate unity, which he terms Omega point. Chardin in this explication stresses the need for people to converge upon each other and to personalize themselves through love. This impetus toward union is designed to effect a convergence of the material and spiritual; we are drawn together in order to merge with Omega, which is incarnated in Christ. But to reach Omega one requires charity, in the Christian sense of *caritas*, an ingredient that is lacking among people in "Everything That Rises Must Converge." Nevertheless, the story radiates beyond the strict enclosure of form because of Chardin's thesis. The entire movement of the story is toward convergence—of black and white, or mother and son—but this convergence is never quite accomplished, although the quest for unity remains an elusive and tantalizing possibility.

Convergence is the process whereby man's tendency toward extreme individuality and disintegration is arrested by a unifying force. Julian, however, is only vaguely aware of this force through the frightening revelation of his mother's death. Flannery O'Connor, following Chardin and other writers of the modern Catholic renaissance such as Romano Guardini, sees great danger in the anti-personalist complex, in the propensity of men to think of themselves as monads which never converge. Man certainly is valuable in his uniqueness, but his spiritual life is contingent upon other considerations. As Chardin explains it,

Egotism, whether personal or racial, is quite rightly excited
by the idea of the element ascending through faithfulness to
life, to the extremes of the incommunicable and the exclusive
that it holds within it. It *feels* right. Its only mistake, but a
fatal one, is *to confuse individuality with personality.* . . .
The goal of ourselves, the acme of our originality, is not our
individuality but our person; and according to the evolution-
ary structure of the world, we can only find our person by
uniting together.[9]

As the world unfolds and as man peels off layer after layer
from his consciousness, he encounters Omega, which is
God, the end of the world. Omega is the emergence of
that which previously was there but was unrealized.
Perception of Omega is consonant with the illumination
which comes from mystical ecstasy, but Julian—like Asbury in "The Enduring Chill"(1958) who is only dimly
aware of the Holy Ghost emblazoned in water stains on
the ceiling of his room—is incapable of realizing the
implications of his revelation. His is a quest which is
incomplete; initiated into a world of suffering, his burden now is to regain equilibrium in a world transformed
by a presence he never knew existed.

Most of Flannery O'Connor's quest protagonists are
attracted by Omega, although the element never sufficiently universalizes itself to be consistently apprehended. Nevertheless, at least one of Miss O'Connor's
investigations of the mystical quest is fully developed. It
is formulated in terms of a quest that is simultaneously
grotesque and mystical, and at the end of the story the
author reveals that through Omega, or illumination, man
can overcome his estranged condition and defeat the
dragon which accosts him. Embarking on a trip to Atlanta,
the two protagonists in "The Artificial Nigger" (1955)
encounter events that are mysterious and painful, but
eventually they learn the nature of grace and the value
of collective humanity. The full complexity and elegance

of this tale certainly is not reflected in Miss O'Connor's laconic account of its origins. Alluding to the title of the story during a symposium held at Vanderbilt University in 1959, she remarked:

> Well, I never had heard the phrase before, but my mother was out trying to buy a cow, and she rode up the country a-piece. She had the address of a man who was supposed to have a cow for sale, but she couldn't find it, so she stopped in a small town and asked the countryman on the side of the road where the house was, and he said, "Well, you go into this town and you can't miss it 'cause it's the only house in town with a artificial nigger in front of it." So I decided I would have to find a story to fit that. A little lower than starting with the theme.[10]

This story is framed in terms of a journey which takes an old man and a boy on an allegorical quest for human identity and communion, a quest which is based largely on Miss O'Connor's close reading of Dante in the early 1950s.[11] Her narrative is a peculiarly modern journey to hell and back, and it is replete with the sort of ludicrousness and horror which many contemporary writers discover in city life. The awakening of self begins in a moon-flooded room where Mr. Head and Nelson are preparing for their journey to Atlanta. The purpose of the awakening of the self is, of course, to develop an awareness of the relationship between man and God, and more often than not this apprehension of the relationship requires an objective correlative, a function served by the presence of the Negro in the story. It is the Negro, evident from the moment that Nelson and Head board the train for Atlanta, who forces the protagonists to recognize suffering and guilt and the need of redemptive grace.

At the beginning of the story both Head and his grandson have disembodied notions of the Negro, since Head
has rarely encountered one and the boy has yet to see
one. The old man associates the Negro with evil, and he
intends to use Nelson's ignorance of the Negro as a
weapon to force humility upon the child. Just as Virgil
alerted Dante to the dangers of hell, so Head warns his
grandson of the evils of the city which, he avers, will be
"full of niggers"; but Nelson, whose hat is literally too
big for him, disdains such advice. Thus it is obvious that
both characters are alerted to the significance of the
Negro, and the entire story then sets out to explore the
enigmas of the subject.

As their journey progresses Nelson and Head move
through a world that is claustrophobic and puzzling. Like
creatures trapped in a maze, they move through a curiously concentric topography which prevents them from
advancing and which intensifies their disorientation. This
motif, which again is reminiscent of the trapped souls in
Dante's hell, begins when Head, in an attempt to maintain
a sense of direction by keeping the dome of the train
terminal in sight, inadvertently circles the area. Once
this circular geography is established, Head and Nelson
move through a constricting series of circles that lead
them deeper and deeper into this metropolitan inferno.
Finally, toward the end of the story, the circular pattern
is reiterated when they enter an exclusive suburban area
and discover that the drives "wound around and around
in endless ridiculous circles." It is this circular pattern
of movement that permits Miss O'Connor to render the
increasing physical and spiritual disorientation of the
characters. As they wander through endless tunnel-like
streets which Head figuratively associates with hell, they
are subjected to a variety of purifying forces — hunger,

heat, and terrifying creatures (including a Medusa-like Negress who turns Nelson to stone) — designed to prepare them for the ultimate moment of illumination.

Movement toward blessedness is excruciating. As they struggle through the city, totally estranged from their environment because of their loss of hope, they encounter a fat man with two bulldogs, a grotesque metamorphosis of the conductor whom they met on the train, who gives them spiritual directions. Having experienced the depths of the dark night of the soul, Nelson and Head are now prepared to receive the mercy of God. This moment of mercy comes when they encounter the artificial nigger: "It was not possible to tell if the artificial Negro were meant to be young or old; he looked too miserable to be either. He was meant to look happy because his mouth was stretched up at the corners but the chipped eye and the angle he was cocked at gave him a wild look of misery instead." The statue is a revelation: it is inscrutable and mysterious, a symbol of universal suffering. Standing before it, Nelson and Head are literally transformed: "Mr. Head looked like an ancient child and Nelson like a minature old man." Both of them are forced to confess to the ultimate mystery of things; both do penance and are purified. The earlier allusion in the story of Raphael coming to Tobiah is now clear: the grandfather and grandson have been taught to rely on God's aid, and His power has been made manifest.

Action in a story like "The Artificial Nigger" is decidedly grotesque: it reveals a sensitivity to those disruptions of modern life which alienate man from his world and from grace. The story — perhaps the most perfect allegory of quest in American literature since Hawthorne wrote "My Kinsman, Major Molineux" — expands from a seemingly realistic narrative of journey to a rounded conception of tragic isolation and moral and spiritual decay. In the end a new Eden is not resurrected, nor is man restored to a prelapsarian state, but he is given a way of saving himself.

The idea of voyage, emphasizing suffering, penance, and piety, thus becomes Flannery O'Connor's ideal form of narrative action. Employed as a metaphor in her fiction, it suggests that all life is essentially a pilgrimage, horrible and dangerous, moving always toward the terrors of damnation or the safety of blessedness. On a purely literal level many of Miss O'Connor's stories trace quests through a world which is potentially chaotic. But at the anagogical level they are journeys involving death, judgment, heaven, and hell. Ultimately the grotesque quest is concerned with these last things; in a story like "The Artificial Nigger," these concerns are treated with remarkable concision and deftness, and the story is great in consequence. As pilgrims Nelson and Head recognize their sins, public and private, and learn to cooperate with grace. The image which they and their counterparts in other stories leave us with is of a geography, a journey of the soul. All O'Connor's characters remind us that our lives are a pilgrimage—and that we go to heaven, or hell, by walking on real roads.

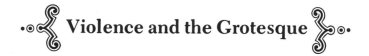

Violence and the Grotesque

Chapter Four Passage in front of the dragon is rarely an orderly event for Flannery O'Connor's protagonists. Although made in the image of God, these pilgrims do not possess perfect vision: they do not realize that the great dragon, who in the Apocalypse of Saint John, the last book in the Bible, is also called the devil, is a powerful adversary, and one who is capable of seducing the entire world. Crippled by faulty reason, these voyagers usually pass into the jaws of this dragon, rather than to a secure home on the far side of danger. They meet with disorientation, destruction, and death. Succumbing to a violence for which they are largely responsible, they discover at the moment of their supreme agony that their relation to the world and to the cosmos has been transformed suddenly by mysterious forces.

Within this context the violence which Miss O'Connor's characters suffer is revelatory. Her restless and tormented offenders are free to destroy themselves, and they frequently do. Like Satan himself they encounter suffering and damnation not because God has predetermined their destruction, but because of their own free will they have abandoned their quest for grace. The outcome of this renunciation is that they find themselves in a chaotic and fallen world. This world is contingent upon the grotesque, and the natural laws which seemingly governed their movements are now threatened by dissolution. And at this point in the narrative movement violence crystallizes the circumstances surrounding their damnation and reveals the extent of their defective natures. The violence inflicted against these travelers forces them to confront the terror of the human condition without God.

Miss O'Connor's technical strategy in the application of violence is to show precisely how the destructive impulse brings the horror of man's grotesque state home to him. Because this kind of violence is religiously motivated, it differs considerably from those gratuitous forms of violence in fiction which are used to exploit current tastes. The violence in Miss O'Connor's fiction is real, yet it has a metaphysical dimension arising from man's loss of theological identity. If in terms of effect this violence partakes of exaggeration, sensationalism, and shock, it nevertheless raises problems which treat the moral and religious order of the universe. The author was quick to distinguish violence in the pure grotesque from its presence in other adulterated forms. She objected to the attempts of some critics to place her within the School of Southern Degeneracy, and she asserted that every time she was associated with this gothic beast she "felt like Br'er Rabbit stuck on the tarbaby."[1] She was emphatic in denying that she utilized violence as a gothic contrivance, remarking that gothicism was a degeneracy which was rarely recognized as such. Fictional assessment of violence in ethical and theological terms is one quality which sets the grotesque apart from a gothic aesthetic, since the violence implicit in gothic fiction has little moral foundation: it exists to satisfy itself, and does not serve as a meaningful vision. Conversely, when violence appears in the grotesque, as in the hecatomb which frames "A Good Man is Hard to Find," it is used to suggest the lack of any framework of order in the universe; it reinforces the grotesque by working *against* the ideals of social and moral order to create an alienated perspective.

It is apparent then that Miss O'Connor places a premium upon violence in her fiction because it is a natural corollary of the grotesque: it creates heightened situations which are not only rich in theological implications but which are also congenial to a grotesque vision. Indeed, since it manifests itself in a world which is always on the verge of disintegration, violence seems to confirm the grotesque. Tales like "Good Country People," "The Life You Save May Be Your Own," and "A Good Man is Hard to Find" harbor violence beneath the surface of the narrative, and it is the eruption of this violence which assures the frigid, unsentimental, and decidedly grotesque tone of O'Connor's fiction. This reinforcement of the grotesque situation with violence is apparent not only in Miss O'Connor, but in many of her southern contempories, whose visions of a dark and incongruous world and of the harsh discontinuities of history are more firmly rooted than those of writers who operate outside of the region. William Faulkner, for one, frequently fused violence and the grotesque; Joe Christmas' emasculation in *Light in August,* and the corncob rape of Temple Drake in the most grotesque of Faulkner's novels, *Sanctuary,* are useful examples of this technique. Robert Penn Warren, who in his concern for the theological foundations of fiction resembles Flannery O'Connor, has employed the method with continual success, most notably in his underrated *World Enough and Time,* an historical novel of the absurd which is replete with murder, rape, and decapitation.

Acts of violence in Miss O'Connor's fiction illuminate a world of continual spiritual warfare. The Misfit in "A Good Man is Hard to Find" kills people not because he enjoys murder, but because like Meursault in *L'Etranger* he is powerless to control his impulses when faced with the indifference of the universe. His act of violence is not totally irrational because its manifestation points toward the spiritual disorder of the world. The Misfit therefore is not presented merely as a pathological murderer, but as a crazed latter-day anchorite, wielding a gun instead of a gnarled club. Still he is without grace, and he complicates the grotesque situation of the Bailey family as well as of himself by ignoring the cardinal commandment—"Thou shalt not kill." Slaughter is a part of the natural process, and modern war demonstrates that it is a part of the human process as well. Yet from a Catholic perspective the injunction placed upon man not to kill is a radical one—and one which must be obeyed. In human and theological terms to kill is to lapse into evil.

Ultimately violence in Flannery O'Connor's fiction forces the reader to confront the problem of evil and to seek alternatives to it. Because Miss O'Connor uses violence to shock her characters (and readers), it becomes the most singular expression of sin within her grotesque landscape. Time and again in her stories violence intrudes suddenly upon the familiar and seemingly secure world and turns the landscape into a secular hell. Thus the slow pastoral seduction planned by Hulga in "Good Country People" is disrupted by Manly Pointer's outrages against her body and spirit. Similarly Julian's world in "Everything that Rises Must Converge" suddenly becomes chaotic when violence ruins what previously had been an innocuous, albeit distasteful, bus trip. Obviously violence of this type occupies a crucial position in making the world seem strange, terrifying, and deprived of grace. As Frederick J. Hoffman remarks in what is perhaps the finest book on violence in contemporary literature: "Surprise is an indispensable element of the fact of violence in modern life. A carefully plotted pattern of expected events has always been needed to sustain a customary existence. A sudden break in the routine challenges the fullest energy of man's power of adjustment. Suddenness is a quality of violence. It is a sign of force breaking through the design established to contain it."[2]

Translated into stylistic terms, the need to make vioence surprising accounts for the deceptively slow pace of many of Flannery O'Connor's stories. As in southwestern humor, a tradition with which she was familiar,[3] Miss O'Connor assumes the role of an impartial and seemingly detached narrator relating a tale which is filled with bizarre and violent action. The deliberately controlled, matter-of-fact omniscience works against the exaggerated effects of the violence to create an incongruity of tone which lends itself to the grotesque. In southwestern humor this technique is known as the "box-like" structure; and when violence exceeds the literary form designed to contain it, there is a suggestion that all characters are susceptible to disruptive forces and to displacement. Not even the sublime scoundrels—the ring-tailed roarers like Sut Lovingood and Simon Suggs —are completely successful in transcending the violence, cruelty, and pain which are characteristic of southwestern fiction. This is true even of George Washington Harris' creation, Sut, who discovers comedy in the discomfort of people whom he does not like and who acts as a scourge to root out the hypocrisy and bestiality in man's nature. Both Sut and Simon are supreme tricksters, and such characters as Tom T. Shiftlet and Manly Pointer are their direct heirs.

To be certain, characters like Shiftlet and Pointer are criminals, yet curiously productive ones, for they are capable of fragmenting a situation through violence and thereby reducing it to absurdity. Through violence they both create the irrationality of their own lives and lead other victims into it. These acts of violence cause relationships to collapse, and they clarify the hatreds, fears, and obsessions of the grotesque antagonists as well. By revealing a world which resists order, the violent antagonist becomes a crucial figure in revealing the nature of the demonic landscape in which he operates.

The violent figure frequently becomes an extension of the world which he inhabits. His spiritual desolation is reflected in the very landscape through which he moves, for in this landscape images of violence and disorder prevail. Flannery O'Connor pays strict attention to scene, to landscape in disarray, because by being a reflection of the interior self of the character, it assumes a complicity, despite its supposedly inanimate nature, in the bizarre disjunctiveness of the universe. The potentially violent and hostile landscape is a mark of Miss O'Connor's fiction and serves as a vivid image of a worldly Inferno. And of course with the author, a violent landscape is almost by extension a grotesque landscape. In other words the reductive power of violence unleashes essentially grotesque currents of feeling. In "A Good Man Is Hard to Find," for instance, the deranged mind of the Misfit, and the secular impulses of a family preordained to destruction, find an objective correlative in images of a distorted and inimical wasteland. The twisted setting in the story mirrors spiritual and moral decay, and the peaceful rhythms usually associated with a family trip are continually undercut by the images of destruction which are juxtaposed against it. Cotton fields with small islands of graves, the dirt road with "sudden washes in it and sharp curves on dangerous embankments," the line of woods which gapes "like a dark open mouth" create a landscape which is menacing and alien. Even the diner which the family stops at for lunch is a precarious structure, lacking any solidarity or harmony, and is presided over by a sadistic monkey which bites fleas between its teeth with delight. Here, and in other stories such as "A Circle in the Fire" (1954) and "A View of the Woods" (1957), the environment impinges upon characters and is potentially violent: physical description consistently works in opposition to people's desire for harmony and order, and it also affords a premonition of disaster.

Flannery O'Connor's technique of description is terse and severe, tending always toward the impressionistic, in which landscape is distilled into primary images which render a picture of a violent physical world. Miss O'Connor, a watercolorist of considerable talent, concentrates upon line and color to evoke locale swiftly; considering the premium which she placed upon the stark outlines of her fiction, any profusion of description would work against her overall narrative intentions, and thus she relied upon the synthetic method of drawing objects in the physical world together to achieve a concentrated effect. Whether describing the countryside or the metropolis, the author is carefully selective and austere, building up a pattern of imagery and frequently counterpointing these images in order to create a charged atmosphere and to make a thematic statement.

One story which is characteristic in its wedding of the violent and grotesque situation to the theological statement is "Greenleaf," which won first place in the O'Henry awards in 1956 and which is one of Miss O'Connor's better stories, unique in its working of materials toward the implications of primitive rather than orthodox Christian myth. The events in this story begin when Mrs. May, owner of a farm, awakes from a disturbing dream in which an unknown presence had devoured her house, family, and lands to discover a bull chewing at the hedge outside her window. The latent violence implicit in the dream and in the activities of the bull, who throughout the story is depicted as a deity and a lover, is rein-

forced by landscape images which convey destructive
potential. This landscape, distilled into the primary image
of the sun, is, like the bull, anathema to Mrs. May, who
is yet another of O'Connor's Great Mothers. The sun is a
dangerous presence: inspecting the milking shed on an
adjacent farm which belongs to the Greenleaf sons, Mrs.
May has the sensation "that the sun was directly on top
of her head, like a silver bullet ready to drop into her
brain." That night she has yet another dream in which,
while striding across her farm, she hears the noise of the
sun, and in this dream the images of the sun and of the
bull merge: "When she first stopped it was a swollen red
ball, but as she stood watching it began to narrow and
pale until it looked like a bullet. Then suddenly it burst
through the tree line and raced down the hill toward her.
She woke up with her hand over her mouth and the same
noise, diminished but distinct, in her ear. It was the bull
munching under the window." Here is a direct analogy
between the bull and another procreative force, indeed
the primal one, the sun. But a fundamental opposition
exists between Mrs. May and the creative forces of nature,
which she regards as hostile and threatening.

Cast into the familiar posture of alienation, Mrs. May
nevertheless refuses to admit to any estrangement from
nature; she merely wants the destructive bull off her
property. Thus she constantly misinterprets her alienation, and fails to perceive the hidden violence of her surroundings, as when she drives out with Mr. Greenleaf,
her tenant, to shoot the bull: "Birds were screaming
everywhere, the grass was almost too bright to look at,
the sky was an even, piercing blue. 'Spring is here,' she
said gaily." In fact nature, heightened and hostile, con-
spires against Mrs. May, for she is a threat to it. When,
for instance, she sees the bull—the symbol of the magical
and mystical forces of nature—grazing peacefully among

the cows, she immediately sends Mr. Greenleaf to shoot him, intent as she is on disrupting the natural environment.

The conclusion of "Greenleaf," enacting a macabre conjugal union between the bull and Mrs. May, is perfect in its archetypal resolutions. Confronted with destruction and (ambiguously) with a penetration that is explicitly sexual, Mrs. May becomes yet another character who is forced out to meet the extremities of her nature. Both she and her gentleman lover "die" together, for Mr. Greenleaf rushes up and shoots the bull in the eye just after he gores Mrs. May. As in many primitive myths, which Miss O'Connor knew from her close reading of Erich Neumann,[4] opposition between male and female forces is reconciled, for Mrs. May is literally embedded in nature at the end of the story. Yet her archetypal fate serves as a model for those who reject their origins in nature and who are insensitive to the spiritual forces which operate within the community.

The landscapes depicted in Flannery O'Connor's fiction seem to intensify man's propensity for physical, psychological, and spiritual violence. In a world deprived of meaning, in a world which is ruthless and cruel, the only consolation which her characters have is an ability to exploit others through violence. Arson, rape, mutilation, suicide, and murder are some of the extremes of violent behavior that appear in O'Connor's fiction, and what is curious about these manifestations is that characters such as Rufus, Shiftlet, and the Bible salesman actually take pleasure in wanton acts of destruction. This pleasure in violence, a phenomenon which preoccupies many behavioral scientists and such philosophers as Karl Jaspers, deprives men of being, although the malefactors believe mistakenly that it serves to define their lives. As such, violence becomes a manifestation of the demonic,

understood in the medieval sense of the word, as a force
which obliterates identity and damns human beings.
Even the Misfit, with his debased logic, comprehends a
world without meaning, and in such a world, where it is
impossible to attach one's loyalties to any overriding
ethical or theological position, the only pleasure and consolation for the lack of meaning must come from amoral
acts of violence. Unlike the Hemingway protagonist, who
attempts to channel violence into such acceptable in-
stitutions as war, hunting, and the bullfight, the characters in O'Connor's fiction rarely seek social justification for their destructive acts. If any justification is re-
quired, it exists in the universe itself, in a fallen and
grotesque world where a perverse Creator forces man to
attest to his damnation every moment of his life.

At the root of violence in Miss O'Connor's fiction lies
this concept of the depraved and potentially lethal world,
in which the destiny of man is seemingly imposed upon
him by a vaguely apprehended source. W. M. Frohock in
The Novel of Violence in America cogently explains the
dilemma which faces the violent protagonist: "The hero
finds himself in a predicament such that the only possible
exit is through inflicting physical harm on some other
human. In the infliction of harm he also finds the way to
his own destruction. But still he accepts the way of violence because life, as he sees it, is like that: violence is
man's fate."⁵ Life—in the existential sense of the word
—is like that, even at the most mundane level. In "The
Displaced Person," for example, the violence is formulated in terms of a basic social opposition between re-
latively established individuals like Mrs. McIntyre and
Mrs. Shortley, and Guizac, who possesses no distinct
social identity but who nevertheless threatens the con-
servative communal patterns of southern farm life. Guizac's own basic rights can be thwarted only by violent

death, yet once this is perpetrated, the world loses its formerly sharp outlines and is transformed into something amorphous and terrifying for those who assumed complicity in Guizac's death.

At the moment of Guizac's death those who are accomplices in it remain remarkably calm and detached, and this failure of response serves to define their grotesque state. As Camus has written in regard to the concentration horrors of this century, "the death or torture of a human being can, in our world, be examined with a feeling of indifference, with friendly or experimental interest, or without response. . . . [And] the putting to death of a man can be regarded other than with the horror and shame it should excite."[6] Guizac, the refugee Pole, whose concentration camp agonies are mirrored in his face, which seems rearranged from broken and disparate parts and held together with pins and wires, expresses the horrors and indignities which men can commit against each other. One act of violence reduces him to a thing, to an object which the farm's inhabitants can observe clinically. This remarkable detachment, a form of the destructive intellect which we have observed in many of O'Connor's less laudable characters, reveals these individuals as fallen creatures, for the violence which they cause illuminates the corruption of their souls.

Because violence undoes most of the characters in "The Displaced Person," the world depicted in this story, as well as the elaborate manners designed to contain the anarchic impulses of individuals, is undercut. In many of her essays Miss O'Connor suggested that manners are the only thing we have to regulate society. Yet in her fiction she tends to give parodies of the novel of manners. There is something macabre and vacuous about social and family relationships in her stories — something not quite credible about her characters' elaborate courtesies. True manners must create social and spiritual harmony. When violence intrudes successfully against manners, or when social conflicts are exacerbated, there has been a failure of manners which has occurred because Miss O'Connor's good country people have lost sight of God.

The entire strategy of violence in Flannery O'Connor's stories of the grotesque is to reveal how complicity in destruction carries men away from God, away from that center of mystery which she was constantly trying to define and which Catholics term grace. This is why violent death is the one act of paramount importance in O'Connor's fiction: it serves to define evil in society. The feud violence which exists in "Greenleaf," for example, is clearly delineated not only in terms of class hatreds but also in terms of good and evil. The pervasive aura of violence in this story reveals the corruption of the will and the need of grace. This kind of violence is a form of spiritual punishment, and in "Revelation," "The Lame Shall Enter First," and many other of her tales it is admonitory. Mrs. May obviously disdains the low origins and primitive ways of the Greenleafs as well as their newly acquired success. With their fox-colored eyes and dark crafty faces they seem to be cast in the mold of Faulkner's tenacious Snopes clan. Yet the Greenleafs, as their name implies, are in basic harmony with nature. More importantly Mrs. Greenleaf embraces a variety of worship which is reminiscent of early mystery religions based on vegetation and on earth. Her mortification and esctasy, which are appalling to Mrs. May, are ways of experiencing the spiritual through nature; moreover, Mrs. Greenleaf thinks in terms of a primitive salvation for mankind. Mrs. May's failure to understand the rituals which Mrs. Greenleaf enacts before her eyes signifies the modern failure to integrate religious mystery with culture. It also explains why Mrs. May's destiny of necessity must be violent, because hers is the fate of the individual who is estranged from the basic forces of the community and from grace.

Another indication of evil in "Greenleaf" is the alienation which exists among the members of the May family. Estrangement within the family is of course one of the most common forms of sublimated violence and overt feuding in Flannery O'Connor's fiction. In "Greenleaf" Mrs. May's two sons loathe their mother and hate each other as well. Wesley, the younger of the brothers, bears spiritual kinship to Hulga, Asbury, and other effete intellectuals who are encountered frequently in Miss O'Connor's stories. He is sickly, sardonic, ill-natured, and rude — a vacuous academician consumed by a brutal sense of determinism. Scofield is much coarser than his brother; patterned after Jason Compson, he displays a marked degeneracy in his manners. Both brothers are perversely preoccupied with their mother's death, and this act suggests how individuals can consciously choose to perform or to wish acts of evil.

Conflict between generations harbors and generates violent behavior. These conflicts are frequently grotesque from the outset because of the strong dependency of the sons upon their mothers, which causes a radical inversion in expected behavior. Characteristically, as in "The Enduring Chill" and "Everything That Rises Must Converge," the mother in these stories represents a masculine principle, whereas the attitude of the son is largely feminine. This motif is apparent in a story which Miss O'Connor published in the *Kenyon Review* in 1960, "The Comforts of Home," which is certainly the most Freudian of her stories. In this piece a son tries to aggrandize the affections of his mother, whose loyalties are divided suddenly between his childlike needs and those of a nymphomaniac whom she has taken into the house in order to reform. Thomas, whose oedipal attachment is rather ludicrous, is terrified of Star Drake the nymphomaniac; appalled by her overtures and disoriented by the chaos which now rules a formerly comfortable home, Thomas threatens petulantly to leave, but never manages to do so. In the end, through his own perverse machinations, Thomas inadvertently shoots his mother with a pistol that he had originally planted in the purse of Star Drake for the sheriff to find.

The conclusion of "The Comforts of Home," with the sheriff gazing at a frozen triangular tableau and imagining a sordid scandal, is a disappointing resolution: it is the only instance in which melodrama tends to exceed the aesthetic structure of the grotesque in Flannery O'Connor's fiction. Yet despite the fact that the pistol — that ambiguous phallic symbol — seems like an excerpt from a case study in sexual neurosis and is utilized in a bald manner alien to her basic techniques, there are subtleties to the story which deserve scrutiny. The best part of the story involves the specter of Thomas's deceased father, a corrupt overbearing man who had possessed influence and power when alive. The father's voice, which controls every step in the son's fatal actions, is associated with the devil, although Thomas refuses to recognize the metamorphosis of that familiar individual in the panama hat: "The old man — small, wasp-like, in his yellowed panama hat, his seersucker suit, his pink carefully-soiled shirt, his small string tie — appeared to have taken up his station in Thomas's mind." Although Thomas is afflicted and eventually possessed by the devil, who leads him into violence, he ironically associates this condition of damnation with his charitable mother: "The devil for Thomas was only a manner of speaking, but it was a manner appropriate to the situations the mother got into.

Had she been in any degree intellectual, he could have proved to her from early Christian history that no excess of virtue is justified, that a moderation of good produces likewise a moderation of evil, that if Anthony in Egypt had stayed at home and attended to his sister, no devils would have plagued him."

Thomas, an historian by training and inclination, disastrously misreads church history and distorts religious doctrine. His mother's "excess of virtue" is merely a willingness to love the lame and the crippled, and in the Kingdom of God there can be no excess of love. Baudelaire termed God a prostitute because He loved everyone; unable to accept this condition, the poet consciously chose evil as an alternative. Similarly Thomas decides to commit evil, and by refusing to acknowledge that mysterious voice in his mind, he performs an act of violence which assures his infernal condition.

For Flannery O'Connor, moral and religious dilemmas cannot be illuminated without violence. As Louise Gossett has observed in her penetrating study of violence in southern fiction, Miss O'Connor makes violence "a religious evaluation of modern life."[7] To be sure, much of the violence in her fiction exists as a negative spiritual quality. Frequently it is utilized as a means of exploitation by amoral individuals, and it induces ruthlessness, cruelty, obsession, and other distortions of mind and matter that contribute to a grotesque perspective. Yet for Flannery O'Connor violence is not necessarily alien to grace; she seemingly sought ways to reconcile the abhorrence of violence in the Old and New Testaments with the reality of Christ coming with a sword and of Elijah slaughtering the prophets of Bael. In short, violence can be used to reinforce an affirmative theological vision when it contends against demonic forces. Rimbaud, who knew perhaps better than any member of his literary generation, remarked that spiritual warfare is as savage as human warfare. The ultimate battle is against evil — and against the devil incarnated in concrete forms — in the figure of a Bible salesman, an old man with a peppermint cane, or a friendly figure in a panama hat. In this situation violence becomes a mark of faith. As the noted historian Jacques Ellul has written: "The whole meaning of the violence of love is contained in Paul's word that evil is to be overcome with good (Romans 12: 17-21). This is a generalization of the Sermon on the Mount. And it is important for us to understand that this sermon shows what the violence of love is. Paul says, 'Do not let yourself be overcome by evil.' This then is the fight — and not only spiritual, for Paul and the whole Bible are very realistic and see that evil is constantly incarnated."[8]

The violence of love is synonymous with faith, and only this sort of violence is effectual in face of the grotesque. Characters like Thomas in "The Comforts of Home" and Hulga in "Good Country People" fail to recognize the true battle. But others accept it reluctantly, undergo violence and suffering, and rage successfully against the absurd. All O'Connor's protagonists are denied basic needs. A few perceive the grotesque nature of the world; they demand recognition of their own worthiness in this world, sense the futility and frustration arising from this need, and consequently embrace what seemingly is the most lucid course of action — violence. In short, whether we are speaking of the Misfit or of Francis Marion Tarwater, this kind of antagonist revolts against an unsatisfactory state of affairs. He indulges in violence because he wants to see if faith can survive. Flannery O'Connor considers all her characters — and the society they compose — as ruled by this harsh geometry of religion. Against the potential framework of religious order she sets violence and disorder, and then she tries to resolve the ambiguity by forcing her characters into those varieties of extreme situation which test the limits of the grotesque. The extreme situation reveals the paradoxical nature of violence in O'Connor's fiction. Young Bevel's drowning in "The River," for instance, permits him a unique salvation, as does the drowning of Bishop in *The Violent Bear It Away.* Guizac's crucifixion in "The Displaced Person" is also his sacrifice for a depraved culture. The Misfit's murders reveal the horror of a world without Christ. The flagellation of O. E. Parker, the physical assaults of Manly Pointer, the depravitives of Rufus Johnson are all examples of violence operating from a shifting and highly ambiguous perspective, for we see in these stories that the infliction of pain and suffering leads to purification and self-knowledge, either for the victimizer or the victim, or for that curious figure, like the Misfit and Shiftlet, Tarwater and Haze Motes, who is both victim and victimizer, who initiates violence only to discover that it rebounds upon him.

At its highest level violence serves as a purgative, as a means of mortification and purification, as a sign of revelation and election, and as a major vehicle of salvation. As such it provides a clue whereby Flannery O'Connor reconciles the grotesque with a Catholic sacramental vision. When, for instance, Haze Motes toward the end of *Wise Blood* subjects himself to extreme penance by filling his shoes with stones, by sleeping with three strands of barbed wire wrapped around his chest, and by deliberately exposing himself to inclement weather, he in effect formulates his own rules of mortification which transform him into an ascetic and a visionary. His frantic attempt to escape the shadow of Jesus—a renunciation that had made his world a nightmare — is now countered by equally vigorous efforts toward union with Christ. No longer does he desire what is delectable, but what is unappealing; this permits purification, and serves as the final prelude in his movement back to Bethlehem. Haze Motes is a typical violent protagonist: the shocks administered to him force an austere drama in which spiritual crisis comes at the moment of physical agony. This effect is apparent in stories like "A Good Man is Hard to Find" and "Parker's Back," and it is clearly evident in *The Violent Bear It Away*, a novel in which language, incident, imagery, and structure are bounded by violence. This novel is a rehearsal of death by drowning, because the crisis in Tarwater's vocation draws inexorably toward a closed circle of water. The struggle in Tarwater's mind to live his own life or to succumb to the forces of mystery is mirrored in the very landscape, which is charged with a spiritual presence that is hostile and inimical to Tarwater's passions, but which sweeps him nevertheless toward his destiny. Finally, in the violent act of drowning, Tarwater compulsively baptizes Bishop as well; death and spiritual rebirth thus are assured through his aggressive behavior.

A dialectic of violence unifies *The Violent Bear It Away*. Not only does this make the novel inherently dramatic, but it permits fresh moral and theological recognitions. This is why Miss O'Connor utilizes the imagery of drowning and of destruction by fire, which have Christian and specifically biblical overtones, to reinforce Tarwater's hopeless struggle against his vocation. Fire — a destructive force — is an especially good correlative to Tarwater's behavior, for it incorporates traditional attitudes toward Christian ritual and liturgy. The orchestration of this motif relies on biblical counterparts: in the Old Testament an angel of the Lord appears to Moses in the form of a burning bush; the prophets are purified by live coals and the burning finger of God; the Israelites are led out of Egypt by a pillar of fire; the fire of God consumes Nadab and Abihu; David is answered by fire; Elijah is taken in a fiery chariot; and the Lord is glorified by fire. And in the New Testament fire is associated with eternal vengeance: John says that the Lord shall baptize with fire; revelations shall be revealed by fire; and fire shall test man's works.

The motif of fire in *The Violent Bear It Away* utilizes many of these biblical parallels. In the novel fire suggests purification, destruction, vengeance, and revelation. Old Tarwater, a hardshell backwoods prophet, "had been burned clean and burned clean again. He had learned by fire." As with the Old Testament prophets the Lord had manifested Himself to the old man in a finger of fire and had seared his blood in the purifying flame. When the old man dies, Francis Marion Tarwater, who had been tutored in prophecy, "expected to see wheels of fire in the eyes of unearthly beasts." Against his great-uncle's expressed commandment the boy sets fire to the cabin, hoping to cremate the body in the flames and thus avoid the trouble of a Christian burial. Renouncing his prophetic calling, Tarwater hastens from the clearing with the sound of flames "moving up through the black night like a whirling chariot." And when he arrives at the city in the middle of the night, the glow of its lights resembles an immense conflagration, and for an instant Tarwater imagines that it is the fire which he has just left. Continually attempting to reject the voice of prophecy, Tarwater moves from woods to city and back to the wilderness, with his path framed by the mysterious force of fire.

At the conclusion of the novel Tarwater destroys and

purifies the place of his defilement at the hands of the mysterious stranger by setting it on fire. Returning to the backwoods clearing, he again sets fire to the woods in an effort to consume his satanic adversary. When he finally learns that Buford Johnson had buried old Tarwater before he had been touched by the flames, the boy has a revelation which assures him of his prophetic mission: "There, rising and spreading in the night, a red-gold tree of fire ascended as if it would consume the darkness in one tremendous burst of flame. The boy's breath went out to meet it. He knew that this was the fire that had encircled Daniel, that had raised Elijah from the earth, that had spoken to Moses and would speak to him." The voice of God comes to Tarwater, who is now purified and strengthened for the mission of prophecy which he must bear with him back to the city of evil. The words of the child evangelist whom both Tarwater and Rayber had heard earlier at a tabernacle sums up the import of his test by fire: " 'The word of God is a burning word to burn you clean, burns man and child, man and child the same, you people! Be saved in the Lord's fire or perish in your own!' "

The spiritual nature of purification by fire is evident in several of Flannery O'Connor's stories. Both "A Circle in the Fire" and "Parker's Back" utilize the fire motif to suggest a purgative force. The episode where Parker drives a tractor into a tree is especially reminiscent of the kind of effect one encounters in *The Violent Bear It Away*:

> He landed on his back while the tractor crashed upside-down into the tree and burst into flame. The first thing Parker saw were his shoes, quickly being eaten by the fire; one was caught under the tractor, the other was some distance away,

> burning by itself. He was not near them. He could feel the
> hot breath of the burning tree on his face. He scrambled
> backwards, still sitting, his eye cavernous, and if he had
> known how to cross himself he would have done it.

Contact with the flaming tree is more than a mere shock
to Parker. Like the book hurled at Ruby Turpin, it induces a revelation, reminiscent of the burning bush
which appeared before Moses. Conscious now of a new
relationship to the world about him, Parker knows that
he is predestined to be victimized, yet paradoxically
saved, by the revelation that has been manifested to
him.

Violence, whether in the form of a burning bush, a
painful tattooing, ritualistic drowning or blinding, or
vindictive assault, illustrates both the pointlessness of a
purely secular world and the indispensable need of God
to correct the absurdity of man's condition. Violence permits individuals to undergo remarkable transformations;
it also contains a sufficient power to rejuvenate a
fallen world. The ambiguous title of *The Violent Bear It
Away* therefore is a sign whereby we can interpret the
capability of violence to resurrect the grotesque world.
The title of the novel derives from the twelfth verse of
Matthew 11, which Miss O'Connor used as an epigraph
to the book: "And from the days of John the Baptist until
now the Kingdom of heaven suffereth violence, and the
violent bear it away." This passage admits to several
primary interpretations, but it seems obvious that Flannery O'Connor employed it in a twofold sense: to suggest that men have always done violence to God's
kingdom, meaning the Christian movement on earth,
and that another form of violence is also operative, a
spiritual force that permits God's kingdom, and consequently a new age, to be realized. Thus, by the end of the

novel, the restatement of Tarwater's prophetic mission
in terms of violence takes on the accents of many reform-
ers, Christian and otherwise, who have striven so
mightily, and in the face of the most savage adversaries,
to plant the true kingdom in the hearts of men.

Revelation of the true kingdom — or, as Miss O'Connor
called it, the true country — is a primary concern in her
fiction, and it is for this reason that she utilized motifs
of violence to get at the incongruous nature of reality
and to reveal the vitality of the grotesque as technique
and vision. In a paragraph that has become a classic statement on the value of the grotesque one can see how the
concept of violence fits into Flannery O'Connor's
vision:

> The novelist with Christian concerns will find in modern
> life distortions which are repugnant to him, and his prob-
> lem will be to make these appear as distortions to an
> audience which is used to seeing them as natural; and he may
> well be forced to take ever more violent means to get his
> vision across to this hostile audience. When you assume that
> your audience holds the same beliefs you do, you can relax
> a little and use more normal ways of talking to it; when you
> have to assume that it does not, then you have to make your
> vision apparent by shock — to the hard of hearing you shout,
> and for the almost-blind you draw large and startling
> figures.[9]

The world of the grotesque, whether we are talking about
O'Connor and Faulkner, Thomas Pynchon and James
Purdy, or Vladimir Nabokov and Jorges Borges, is a
world of distortions — in character and landscape and also
in spirit. Demonic and violent acts therefore are a means
whereby we can fix the precise limits of meaning in this
alien and mysterious world. At the same time violence
becomes a source of hope whereby man can transcend

his grotesque condition. As Miss O'Connor has written in reference to "A Good Man Is Hard to Find":

> We hear many complaints about the prevalence of violence in modern fiction, and it is always assumed that this violence is a bad thing and meant to be an end in itself. With the serious writer, violence is never an end in itself. It is the extreme situation that best reveals what we are essentially, and I believe these are times when writers are most interested in what we are essentially, than in the tenor of our daily lives. Violence is a force which can be used for good or evil, and among the things taken by it is the kingdom of heaven. But regardless of what can be taken by it, the man in the violent situation reveals those qualities least dispensable in his personality, those qualities which are all he will have to take into eternity with him; and since the characters in this story are all on the verge of eternity, it is appropriate to think of what they take with them.[10]

In the broadest sense, to reflect on the grotesque is to reflect upon violence: essentially the modern condition reveals that violence creates a perilous balance between the horrifying and the ludicrous. Flannery O'Connor knew that the grotesque, by descending into the claustral world of violence, of the incongruous and irrational, contains within itself the germ whereby a transcendent order can be discovered: in an ambiguous world you look for absolutes, and when you face the unknown you invariably recognize spiritual mystery. Violence speaks to us about our experience of such a world by revealing the human need for something beyond a purely secular vision.

 **The Catholic Grotesque**

Chapter Five   Concentration upon violence, suffering, and disorder—upon those concepts that are integral parts of a grotesque vision—forced Flannery O'Connor to accept the ultimate complexity of things and to come to terms with human motivations as they relate to the problem of sustaining a significant faith. Like such writers as Dostoevsky and George Bernanos she wanted to explore the manner in which grace complements suffering humanity. As she described this relationship in a 1958 postcard to Katherine Anne Porter from Lourdes, where she had gone for a holy pilgrimage: "The sight of Faith and affliction joined in prayer, very impressive."[1] Miss O'Connor relies on Christian doctrine to explain the agonies of the world because she understands, as do many writers of Catholic origin in modern times, that it is geared to problems of sin and evil, life and death, happiness and despair. In other words she utilizes Catholic and broadly Christian doctrines to illuminate emotions and experiences that emerge from a grotesque perspective. She is an artist of the Catholic grotesque, and therefore acknowledges possibilities of meaning which transcend the ordinary configurations of the secular grotesque. Her fiction provides a way by which the grotesque can be tested and evaluated, accepted or rejected, in a Christian light. She realizes that Christianity can be effective ethically as an antidote to the grotesque, for the moral values of Christianity, emphasizing justice, equality, and charity, can be transposed into values which are lacking in culture but which must be restored if the condition of the absurd is to be overcome. Miss O'Connor once wrote that the Bible "is what we share with all Christians, and the Old Testament we share with all Jews. This is sacred history and our mythic background. If we are going to discard this we had better stop writing at all."[2] The author did not discard her heritage; instead she utilized it as a foundation for her own fiction by merging Christianity with the emotional and ethical dilemmas of her characters – a wedding that creates the distinctive tone of her fiction.

Cast adrift in the world of the grotesque, the characters in Flannery O'Connor's fiction invariably are inducted into the dimensions of sin and evil. Miss O'Connor would have agreed with Cardinal Newman, who observed that any profoundly spiritual literature in modern times would have to be a chronicle of sin. This is why her characters are so unique and irreplaceable: they are marked by God for the most agonizing and unusual adventures, and they harbor destinies that reveal an unusual accretion of evil and sin. As the conditions of disorder and damnation, spawned by the grotesque, unfold, so too do the ways of grace. Yet here Miss O'Connor is no ingénue. Her dark preoccupations rarely permit a benevolent God, but rather a severe and demanding one. This mysterious presence stands poised over the landscape of the grotesque, ready to wreak vengeance on people in their eternal flight from religious responsibilities. This is to say that when the author explores the ways which grace works in the world of the absurd, she does not accomodate herself to benign theological visions. "As Catholics," she wrote, "we are interested in grace, but we should not be so prone to ignore how very divisive grace is; we should not so often forget that it cuts with the sword Christ said He came to bring."[3]

The terrorized flight of O'Connor's characters from God turns them into sinners in a moral and theological sense. As Peguy remarked, the sinner is at the heart of Christianity, for no one knows as much about Christianity as the sinner, unless it is the saint. There are no saints in O'Connor fiction, but here is an incredible legion of sinners, because in her stories the Catholic universe of evil is presented. Miss O'Connor wrote Christian, explicitly Catholic stories about the grotesque, in which men are activated in obscure, seemingly demonic ways. There is real tragic potential in this theme of sin, but only rarely, as in "The Displaced Person," does the tenor of her fiction approach pure tragedy: usually an implicitly somber theme is undercut by the accretion of humor to the materials and by the almost exaggerated heartiness in the way many of these sinners revel in their malfeasance. Of course, Miss O'Connor was an artist devoted to a particular vision of life and to a specific Catholic faith which she pursued with fidelity and increasing skill. Yet although her stories turn upon problems of religious orthodoxy and the orientation of her fiction — the very life of it — is given its directions by a theological interpretation of reality, there is no conventional Christian piety in her work. Whenever Christian piety does appear, it is an object of chilling satire and travesty: in other words it is transformed into a comic and inherently absurd view of life, as when Ruby Turpin in "Revelation," considering her position in God's world, expresses her gratitude for the fact that the Lord has not made her a Negro or poor white trash.

The method of Miss O'Connor's fiction is in fact far more complicated than those of many Christian novelists bent on presenting a sacramental vision. Having committed herself to investigating the vagaries of the grotesque, she did not believe that a vision of sin should be projected solely for the propagation of the faith, but because it retained a fidelity to the truths of reality. "My own feeling," she observed, "is that writers who see by the light of their Christian faith will have in these times, the sharpest eye for the grotesque, for the perverse, and for the unacceptable."[4] The grotesque by its very definition inhibits the possibility of Christian tragedy, but it does not expunge the possibility of making a Christian statement about the nature of reality. All her fiction is an assault on the common man's submission to the forces of the grotesque. Flannery O'Connor seeks to overcome the grotesque with grace — or to strike a perilous balance between the two. It is as though discord demands harmony, as though the lacerations caused by violence, madness, and the inexplicable require an extraordinary solution.

O'Connor's absurd tricksters and grotesque Christ figures take on the sins of the world, but their agonies are not mere retellings of absolute misery and prolonged nightmare ending in death. For the gallows humor which permeates her fiction has its more serious side. As a Catholic, Miss O'Connor believed in original sin, judgment, mercy, and revelation. Her fiction places an extreme emphasis on these features, on what she termed "preoccupations with belief and with death and grace and the devil."[5] In the interview where this statement appears, the author elaborates upon one of these features that is especially apparent in her fiction. "I'm a born Catholic," she says, "and death has always been brother to my imagination. I can't imagine a story that doesn't properly end in it or in its foreshadowing."[6] As traced in the preceding chapters, much of her fiction, generated by varieties of violence, ends in a death which is either literal or figurative. Her interest in the sheer demonic as it is reflected in images of destruction and death is perhaps a literary obsession, but one which reveals a genuine concern with the problem of erecting a faith that can combat the grotesque. Miss O'Connor is not, however, as John Hawkes and others have asserted, a demonist too much in love with her materials. If she concentrates on death and on horror that can be alleviated only by comic interludes, it is because the crisis for her characters is between nature and grace; born into original sin, they are thwarted in their efforts to achieve complete autonomy. In their fierce rebellions they frequently lapse into the demonic, which as Kayser remarks is the essence of the grotesque vision. For Flannery O'Connor the demonic is not a variety of sorcery, but rather a type of Christian heresy, a theological crime. It is the foremost manifestation of evil, an evil designed to destroy God's kingdom on earth. The demonic thus involves not only the grotesque world but also a denial of God in the minds and motives of men. This occurs because many of her characters are either possessed by or obsessed with the devil. The devil, in other words, either inhabits the minds of her characters, or besieges them. The devil, representative of supreme evil, enters into pacts with people, and once he afflicts their wills he can induce various forms of derangement and damnation.

The demonic, which serves to define the grotesque, is rooted in scripture and in Jewish apocalyptic literature. Probably the legend of the fall of Satan led to the investigation of the problem of evil and of the demonic in a depraved world. Historically in Catholicism the demon who possesses men's souls can be beneficent or malevolent, but the mode of his operations in Flannery O'Connor's fiction is always malignant and has evil connotations. Thus she stands within a tradition in American literature which extends back to Cotton Mather, who spoke of demonism in this negative sense, as "the doing of strange and for the most part ill things by the help of evil spirits."

Misfortunes caused by unknown forces, by inexplicable and disastrous events, thus have their explanation in the demonic, in the *maleficia* of satanic creatures who perform acts of evil because they delight in causing suffering and injury. Conjurations of the demonic abound in O'Connor's fiction, and the devil's imprint can be found in a considerable amount of her narrative. The metamorphoses of the devil in *The Violent Bear It Away*, which has an authority stretching back to Aquinas, is merely one indication of the ways by which demonical possession can afflict a person.

Agreements with the devil—as with Rufus Johnson and Haze Motes—are also common in Flannery O'Connor's fiction, and only those who are capable of exorcising the demonic influence are capable of perceiving grace. Exorcism, which is still practiced by the Catholic church, is the only cure for those possessed demonically. Growing out of the New Testament, it provides a way by which man can regain control over his own soul. This ritual of exorcism, which is apparent in such stories as "The River" and "Parker's Back," as well as in both of O'Connor's novels, constitutes a means of purification whereby men can prepare themselves for the manifestation of grace.

Sooner or later all of her characters encounter the presence of grace, the holiness of the secular. Miss O'Connor, by concentrating on the extreme grotesque, reinforces a notion which Bernanos stated poignantly in his diary: grace is everywhere. It is unavoidable, even in the world of the demonic, and because of it the absurd hero, the penultimate example of unredeemed man, is never absolved of violence or complicity in evil. Flannery O'Connor deals with mortal sins—with murder, betrayal, renunciation, and blasphemy—and with ultimate problems involving death, judgment, heaven and hell, because she realizes that it is the strength of sinners which instills

grace — and Christianity — with its importance. She knew,
moreover, that such religious terms could be made artis-
tically viable and that they could easily be converted into
psychological and social analogues through the application of the techniques of the grotesque.

The dramatic value of grotesque technique and vision
is actually what permits Flannery O'Connor to present
her theological vision convincingly. "Part of the complexity of the problem for the Catholic fiction writer,"
she acknowledged, "will be the presence of grace as it
appears in nature, and what matters for him here is that
his faith not become detached from his dramatic sense
and from his vision of what-is."[7] Miss O'Connor realized
that to talk about evil and grace in the kind of world in
which we live requires extraordinary techniques and
effects, as the charitable gesture of the grandmother toward the Misfit prior to her liquidation suggests.[8] Grace
has to be rooted in the ordinariness of life, but violence
and shock can not be abjured in making grace dramatically acceptable. As the author remarked, this is a desperate remedy, but one which is necessary to impress the
deaf, dumb, and blind.

Referring to James's classic dictum that morality in
fiction was directly related to the amount of felt life it
projected, Miss O'Connor reaffirmed that the Catholic
writer "will feel life from the standpoint of the central
Christian mystery: that it has, for all its horror, been
found by God to be worth dying for."[9] She realized that
the vitality of the grotesque resides in the familiar world
which is transformed, and for her this alteration must be
associated with religious mystery. In a letter to William
Van O'Connor she wrote, "It seems to me that the grotesque can have no meaning in fiction unless it is seen or
felt in relation to what is right and normal. My own belief
about what is morally right and normal comes from

Christian orthodoxy; comes from believing that Christ should be the center of life and of the individual soul; whereas the most obvious thing about the society I live in and write about is that Christ is hardly the center of it."[10]

Flannery O'Connor seemingly discovered her natural idiom in stories which embody all the temporal inanities of the grotesque but whose deepest resonance comes from the accretion of theological overtones that are inseparable from the concrete matrix of the story. In other words the writer who shares O'Connor's concerns must force reality out to the limits of mystery: "Such a writer will be interested in what we don't understand rather than in what we do. He will be interested in possibility rather than probability. He will be interested in characters who are forced out to meet evil and grace and who act on a trust beyond themselves — whether they know very clearly what it is they act upon or not."[11] She amplifies this important point in yet another essay:

> When fiction is made according to its nature, it should reinforce our sense of the supernatural by grounding it in concrete observable reality. If the writer uses his eyes in the real security of his Faith, he will be obliged to use them honestly, and his sense of mystery, and his acceptance of it, will be increased. To look at the worst will be for him no more than an act of trust in God....
>
> A belief in fixed dogma cannot fix what goes on in life or blind the believer to it. It will, of course, add a dimension to the writer's observation which many cannot, in conscience, acknowledge exists, but as long as what they *can* acknowledge is present in the work, they cannot claim that any freedom has been denied the artist. A dimension taken away is one thing, a dimension added is another; and what the Catholic writer and reader will have to remember is that the reality of the added dimension will be judged in a work of fiction by the truthfulness and wholeness of the

natural events presented. If the Catholic writer hopes to reveal mysteries, he will have to do it by describing truthfully what he sees from where he is. An affirmative vision cannot be demanded of him without limiting his freedom to observe what man has done with the things of God.[12].

It is Miss O'Connor's emphasis on a precise transcription of the concrete that carries the theological density of her fiction to a consistent and convincing conclusion. According to her this type of fiction, which attempts to combine the concrete and the invisible, "is going to be wild, . . . it is almost of necessity going to be violent and comic, because of the discrepancies that it seeks to combine." This fiction will inevitably be grotesque, but not sentimental, as in gothic fiction, for "intellectual and moral judgments implicit in it shall have the ascendency over feeling." This suggests that the writer of such fiction is interested in grotesque characters and situations because he wants to cultivate a prophetic vision: "In the novelist's case, prophecy is a matter of seeing near things with their extensions of meaning and thus of seeing far things close up. The prophet is a realist of distances, and it is this kind of realism that you find in the best modern instances of the grotesque."[13] The movement in Flannery O'Connor's fiction is from the concrete to the mysterious, since she continually stresses the necessity of seeing through observable reality to the transcendent. To accomplish this task, the writer must possess a special attitude toward the problems of perception. As Miss O'Connor remarked in "The Church and the Fiction Writer":

For the writer of fiction, everything has its testing point in the eye, an organ which eventually involves the whole personality and as much of the world as can be got into it.

Msgr. Romano Guardini has written that the roots of the eye are in the heart. In any case, for the Catholic they stretch far and away into those depths of mystery which the modern world is divided about—part of it trying to eliminate mystery while another part tries to rediscover it in disciplines less personally demanding than religion.[14]

To penetrate that area of mystery which such writers as Flannery O'Connor see at the core of reality, the artist must be a visionary—not in the sense that he can predict the future—but in that he can discern those forces which create mystery in existence. For a Christian, of course, these forces are spiritual, and they are polarized between God and that formidable adversary, Satan. It was the prophets—Amos, Micah, Josiah, Christ—who were in touch with the mainstreams of reality and of action. They lived with mystery and knew that a prophetic view of life enhanced the worth and dignity of man, even as it withheld salvation from those who allied themselves with the demonic forces of nonbeing. Miss O'Connor believed in the prophetic nature of life, and felt that a main obligation of the writer was to illuminate the connection between prophecy and action:

> The writer's gaze has to extend beyond the surface, beyond mere problems, until it touches the realm of mystery which is the concern of prophets. True prophecy in the novelist's case is a matter of seeing near things with their extensions of meanings and thus of seeing far things close up. If a writer believes that the life of man is and will remain essentially mysterious, what he sees on the surface, or what he understands, will be of interest to him only as it leads him into experience of mystery itself. As we make more and more discoveries about ourselves, we push the limits of fiction farther and farther outward.[15]

As the author remarked on several occasions, the prophetic writer, the realist of distances, is the most significant variety of novelist in modern times. By scrutinizing things close up, Miss O'Connor, who cast herself in this tradition, was forced to seek objects that could radiate outward in meaning to the point of mystery that she was trying to reveal: a peacock, a dilapidated car, a statue of a Negro, a tattoo of a Byzantine Christ. All these objects are discrete particulars existing in a concrete world. Yet in the context of O'Connor's fiction they succeed in creating an effect which combines disengagement from the finite world of the story with a prolongation of the theological—and hence mysterious—consequences produced. This effect is extremely hard to bring off without lapsing into mere facileness. It is a technique Miss O'Connor learned, I suspect, from her close reading of Hawthorne, a writer whom she valued highly and who influenced her significantly.

In the fiction of both writers objects are charged with mystery. Thus the exotic peacock in "The Displaced Person" distinguishes this story from other Christ fables like Melville's superlative "Bartleby" or the more contrived A Fable by Faulkner, because it generates a second theological meaning which counterpoints the figure of Guizac in an inventive and technically successful manner. The peacock appears in the first sentence of the story, and the attitudes of the characters toward its physical splendor serve as an index of their attitude toward Guizac as well. Mrs. McIntyre, preoccupied with the secular pursuit of wealth, sees in the peacock another mouth to feed, and she tolerates the bird, the last of an original brood of twenty, only because her deceased husband, the judge, loved them. To Mrs. Shortley the peacock seems like any other domestic fowl, lacking in any extraordinary beauty or grace. In significant contrast to the women Father Flynn is immediately enthralled by the beauty of the bird. In his first encounter with the peacock he envisions it "as if he had just come down from some sun-drenched height to be a vision for them all." Later in the story, when the priest resists Mrs. McIntyre's threat to displace Guizac, he takes consolation in the physical presence of the peacock: "The cock stopped suddenly and curving his neck backwards, he raised his tail and spread it with a shimmering timbrous noise. Tiers of small pregnant suns floated in a green gold haze over his head." It is precisely at this juncture that the peacock as Christ—and Guizac as Christ—merge, for Father Flynn, himself transfigured by the splendor of Christ as revealed in the peacock, mistakes Mrs. McIntyre's reference to Guizac—"'He didn't have to come in the first place'"—and replies absently, "'He came to redeem us.'"

Flannery O'Connor always disliked the loaded term "symbolism," and she often alluded to critics who, in her own idiom, strain the soup too thin; yet it is easy to see that the peacock, which is not interchangeable with any other object, adds a considerable power to the story. There is a longstanding tradition in Christian iconography and symbolism in which the peacock serves as a figuration of Christ. Miss O'Connor compounds this inherited symbol with that of the Displaced Person in an effort to present a complete narrative of the Christian experience, centered on the theme of displacement. Just as Guizac is representative of the historical Christ, the peacock implies a Christ transcendent and divine. The radiant beauty of the peacock thus becomes an abstraction in a way which Guizac does not, because the peacock is a purely religious symbol, not a cultural one. Therefore, as an empirical object, its aspect expresses the transcendent. The peacock is even more mysterious than Guizac; yet it is not detached from the historical context, because the legend of the displaced Christ is absorbed into the transcendent, as the author had intended.

These liturgical objects, whether a peacock in "The Displaced Person," a water stain in "The Enduring Chill," or a tattoo in "Parker's Back," permit Flannery O'Connor to neutralize the world of the grotesque and to clarify those mysteries which serve as an antidote to it. However, mysteries do not simplify the world; suffering and death still remain, but as she remarked in her postcard from Lourdes, affliction is now wedded to a spiritual faith. It is the interrelation of the grotesque and the holy that Miss O'Connor was primarily concerned with in working out the lineaments of her fictive universe, and the illumination of this relationship came more often than not at unexpected moments. The hermaphrodite, for instance, in "A Temple of the Holy Ghost" (1954), is one of those objects radiating mystery, for he connects his grotesque agonies with a deeper spiritual order. As he says, in what reads as an apostrophe to O'Connor's fiction, and indeed to her own life: "'God made me this-away and if you laugh he may strike you the same way. This is the way He wanted me to be and I ain't disputing His way. I'm showing you because I got to make the best of it. I expect you to act like ladies and gentlemen. I never done it to myself nor had a thing to do with it but I'm making the best of it. I don't dispute hit.'" By confronting these dark apocalyptic images of pain in Miss O'Connor's fiction, we are forced to acknowledge both the satanic nature of the world and the necessity of radically transforming it. Thus, as she once said, the grotesque becomes our desperate answer to man's agonizing condition, because through it we are initiated into the holiness of the secular.

What is particularly remarkable about Flannery O'Connor's fiction is this affirmativeness of the grotesque vision. It is almost as though she was born to appreciate the grotesque, for suffering and the inexplicable are at the center of her universe. Miss O'Connor selects and carefully develops details in such a way that a complicated conception of man emerges. Preoccupied with the crisis of belief in the modern age, she saw this crisis manifested in the absurd fever of denial, loneliness, isolation, and alienation—in all those demonic forces which animate characters and drive them relentlessly toward their fate. Her fiction, of course, reveals a commitment in face of the grotesque: the appalling journeys which she forces upon her characters do not end at the point of disorder and nightmare, but radiate outward toward a Catholic sacramental vision of life. This fusion of grotesque vision and theological vision suggests O'Connor's greatest literary gift—her ability to shape reality convincingly to orthodox Christianity.

The absurd agonies of Miss O'Connor's characters present a penetrating critique of the purposelessness of existence without God, and although there are no plenary indulgences in her fiction, her final image of man is a temperate one. She is at once struck by man's roguish capacity for sin and his capacity for salvation. Her characters owe their existence to something outside themselves; rarely are they God's highest creatures, but nevertheless they seem to articulate perfectly the metaphysical possibilities of salvation or damnation. And this tension illuminates the fundamental mystery of all creation, wherein even the lowest are capable of election. This is the burden in one of the most extraordinary passages in Flannery O'Connor's fiction, Ruby Turpin's revelation:

> There was only a purple streak in the sky, cutting through a field of crimson and leading, like an extension of the

highway, into the descending dusk. She raised her hands
from the side of the pen in a gesture hieratic and profound.
A visionary light settled in her eyes. She saw the streak as a
vast swinging bridge extending upward from the earth
through a field of living fire. Upon it a vast horde of souls
were rumbling toward heaven. There were whole companies
of white-trash, clean for the first time in their lives and bands
of black niggers in white robes, and battalions of freaks and
lunatics shouting and clapping and leaping like frogs. And
bringing up the end of the procession was a tribe of people
whom she recognized at once as those who, like herself and
Claud, had always had a little of everything and the God-
given wit to use it right. She leaned forward to observe them
closer. They were marching behind the others with great
dignity, accountable as they always had been for good order
and common sense and respectable behavior. They alone
were on key. Yet she could see by their shocked and altered
faces that even their virtues were being burned away. She
lowered her hands and gripped the rail of the hog pen, her
eyes small but fixed unblinkingly on what lay ahead. In a
moment the vision faded but she remained where she was,
immobile.

This is no place to argue over the validity of visions.
What is significant here is the tolerance of the artist
toward all humanity. In her introduction to *A Memoir of
Mary Ann* Miss O'Connor wrote: "This action whereby
charity grows among us, entwining the living and the
dead, is called by the Church the Communion of Saints.
It is a communion created upon human perfection, created from what we make of our grotesque state.[16] Her
vast horde of souls thus speaks to us from the center of
the Christian experience. Here is a Christian presentation of anxiety, despair, and disorder, unique in modern
American fiction, a fiction which traditionally has had
recourse to extreme vision.

Flannery O'Connor was a visionary—admittedly a
comic one—whose powers of perception made both secular and religious experience more meaningful. She

hated evil with an intensity and clarity of insight unusual among modern writers, who are frequently seduced by the attractiveness and fascination of evil. Her art was not moribund at the time of her death. Caroline Gordon, who visited Miss O'Connor in the Milledgeville hospital a few weeks before her death, recalls a notebook which she kept under her pillow. In it she was trying to complete her final story, "Parker's Back." The doctor, she wryly remarked, had advised her that writing was an acceptable pastime; it was not, he assured her, an exhausting activity. Yet writing and revision had always come hard for Miss O'Connor, even during her healthier periods at Andalusia farm. We can only feel wonderment for the merit of her last story – and for the purity of vision of the woman who wrote it. The story derives from her classic motif of men raging against the General, and it continues to stress the *via negativa*. Yet here we see new imaginative materials, and the injection of a new theme stressing the necessity of humility as the expense of blessedness. This story, which ranks with "The Displaced Person" and "The Artificial Nigger" as her greatest, adds to the one tribute to her craft that Flannery O'Connor always cherished the most: that in uncovering the mysterious workings and compulsions of the human soul, she had succeeded in telling a good story.

Notes to Chapter One

1. "The King of Birds," in *Mystery and Manners*, ed. Sally and Robert Fitzgerald (New York: Farrar, Straus & Giroux, 1969), p. 4. This essay, which first appeared in *Holiday* (September 1961), should be read carefully, for it reveals significant aspects of Miss O'Connor's art and the form in which she cast it.

2. "The Grotesque: An American Genre," *The Grotesque and Other Essays* (Carbondale: Southern Illinois Univ. Press, 1962), pp. 1–19. Aside from a certain looseness in definition, this essay is one of the few incisive analyses of the grotesque in American literature.

3. *The Grotesque in Art and Literature*, trans. Ulrich Weisstein (Bloomington: Indiana Univ. Press, 1963), p. 19. Although literary critics have largely ignored the grotesque as a genre or art form, a considerable amount of spade work has been performed by art historians such as Kayser. In this connection, books by Erwin Panofsky (*Gothic Architecture and Scholasticism*, Latrobe, Penn.: Archabbey Press, 1951), Emîle Mâle (*The Gothic Image*, New York: Harper, 1958), and Otto von Simson (*The Gothic Cathedral*, New York: Harper, 1956) are most useful in exploring the medieval foundations of the grotesque. As for the art of the grotesque during the past two centuries, Kayser's book remains the most intelligent investigation of the subject. This study may be profitably supplemented by Arthur Clayborough's *The Grotesque in English Literature* (Oxford: Clarendon Press, 1965); by Lee Jennings' *The Ludicrous Demon* (Berkeley: Univ. of California Press, 1963); and by the first chapter in Alfred Appel, Jr.'s *A Season of Dreams* (Baton Rouge: Louisiana State Univ. Press, 1965).

4. T. Tindall Wildridge, *The Grotesque in Church Art* (London: W. Andrews, 1899), p. 23.

5. *Gothic Architecture and Scholasticism* (Latrobe, Pennsylvania: Archabbey Press, 1951), p. 64.

6. This brief summary scarcely does justice to a major tradition in American fiction. Either in pure or hybrid form, the grotesque appears in the work of most of our major writers. What we might term the theological grotesque is evident in Hawthorne (but only in those stories—for instance "My Kinsman, Major Molineux"—where there is an inordinate amount of demonic laughter), in certain works by Melville (notably *The Confidence-Man*), in Nathanael West, Djuna Barnes, Robert Penn Warren, J. F. Powers, and of course Miss O'Connor. The secular grotesque can be traced from the southwestern humorists to most contemporary fiction writers like Purdy and Hawkes. Moreover with our most complex novelists—for example Melville and Nabokov—

the grotesque merges with the art of involution, in which the reader himself is drawn into the writer's absurd vision.

7. *The Myth of Sisyphus and Other Essays*, trans. Justin O'Brien (New York: Knopf, 1961), p. 22.

8. *The Grotesque in Art and Literature*, pp. 184, 185, 187, 188.

9. *The Theatre of the Absurd* (London: Hubert Wilson, 1962), p. 300. Esslin uses the words "grotesque" and "absurd" interchangeably, a procedure which is—as I have tried to demonstrate in this chapter— quite proper. Mr. Esslin's final two chapters, in which he traces the evolution of the absurd in European drama, provide superlative commentary on this genre.

10. Quotations from Miss O'Connor's fiction are taken from the standard editions of her novels and stories; these appear in the acknowledgment paragraph on the copyright page of the present study. For those interested in further primary and secondary bibliographical information on Flannery O'Connor, readers should consult the excellent compilation at the end of M. J. Friedman and L. A. Lawson's *The Added Dimension: The Mind and Art of Flannery O'Connor* (New York: Fordham Univ. Press, 1966), pp. 283–302.

11. C. Ross Mullins, "Flannery O'Connor: An Interview," *Jubilee*, 11 (June 1963), 34.

12. Typical of this confusion are essays by William Esty ("In America, Intellectual Bomb Shelters," *Commonweal*, 67, March 7, 1958, 586–88) who speaks of the "cult of the gratuitous grotesque," and Robert O. Bowen ("Hope vs. Despair in the New Gothic Novel," *Renascence*, 13, Spring 1961, 147–52) who makes the same mistake that more thorough critics like Irving Malin do in failing to distinguish between the gothic and the grotesque.

13. The problem of separating the grotesque from that of surrealism is, as this brief paragraph suggests, an extremely delicate one, and one which in certain respects admits to no division because of the coincidence of form (and sometimes even vision) in the two. Readers who wish to pursue this question further should consult Wallace Fowlie's *Age of Surrealism* (New York: Swallow Press, 1950) and J. H. Matthews' *An Introduction to Surrealism* (University Park: Pennsylvania State Univ. Press, 1965).

14. "The Geranium," *Accent*, 4 (Summer 1946), 252. Subsequent references to this uncollected story are given parenthetically in the text. The city as nightmare is a major contemporary landscape in American literature, and this distopian vision can be traced in such representative works as Nathanael West's *The Day of the Locust*, Ralph Ellison's *Invisible Man*, Saul Bellow's *Seize the Day*, and Thomas Pynchon's *V*.

Notes to Chapter Two

1. "Flannery O'Connor—A Tribute," *Esprit*, 8 (Winter 1964), 33. This issue of the magazine, published at the University of Scranton, is a special memorial edition to Flannery O'Connor. It contains some fifty appreciations of Miss O'Connor by writers and critics, many of whom knew the author personally.

2. *Flannery O'Connor*, University of Minnesota Pamphlets on American Writers, No. 54 (Minneapolis: Univ. of Minnesota Press, 1966), p. 43.

3. "Some Aspects of the Grotesque in Southern Literature," in *Mystery and Manners*, ed. Sally and Robert Fitzgerald (New York: Farrar, Straus & Giroux, 1969), p. 43. This essay was published originally in *Cluster Review* (March 1965). Miss O'Connor was one of the few writers of the grotesque who commented on the tradition and genre which she was using in her fiction.

4. Ibid., p. 42.

5. "Flannery O'Connor—A Tribute," p. 23.

6. *Wise Blood* (New York: Farrar, Straus & Giroux, 1962).

7. John Hawkes, "Flannery O'Connor's Devil," *Sewanee Review*, 70 (Summer 1962), 400. Hawkes and Miss O'Connor were friends and mutual admirers of each other's fiction. The similarity in grotesque technique and vision in these two writers merits further investigation.

8. Cyrus Hoy and Walter Sullivan, eds., "An Interview with Flannery O'Connor," *Vagabond*, 4 (February 1960); rpt. in *Writer to Writer*, ed. Floyd C. Watkins and Karl F. Knight (New York: Houghton Mifflin, 1966), pp. 87–88.

9. Joel Wells, "Off the Cuff," *Critic*, 21 (August 1962), 72.

10. For an excellent discussion of these symbols see Sister M. Joselyn, O.S.B., "Thematic Centers in 'The Displaced Person,'" *Studies in Short Fiction*, 1 (Winter 1964), 85–92.

11. *Mystery and Manners*, pp. 196–97. This essay appeared initially in the Georgetown magazine, *Viewpoint* (Spring 1966).

12. Ibid., p. 54. "The Regional Writer" was first published in *Esprit*, 7 (Winter 1963).

13. Ibid., p. 103.

14. "The Southern Temper," in *Southern Renascence*, ed. Louis D. Rubin, Jr., and Robert D. Jacobs (Baltimore: Johns Hopkins Press, 1953), p. 11. Many of the most astute critics of southern literature have acknowledged this holiness of the secular. See in this anthology the essays by Richard Weaver and Andrew Lytle, and in the editors' *South:*

Modern Southern Literature in its Cultural Setting (Garden City: Doubleday, 1961) the essay by Louise Cowan, who writes: ". . . as a community adapts itself to a way of life, a conciliation of the divine and the human orders may be effected within it. In such a society, economic, moral, and aesthetic patterns, transformed by a kind of grace, lose their exclusively secular character and begin to assume a sacredness within the community; and loyalty between members of the community rests on this essentially metaphysical basis. Men do not bow to each other but to the divine as it manifests itself in the communal life" (pp. 98–99).

15. "The Fiction Writer and His Country," in *The Living Novel: A Symposium*, ed. Granville Hicks (New York: Collier, 1957), p. 163.

16. "The Southern Writer and the Great Literary Secession," *Georgia Review*, 24 (Winter 1970), 393–412. As with Heilman and others Simpson connects the posture of the literary exile with manifestations of the divine. "The vision of the Agrarians," he writes, "always had . . . a strong religious and metaphysical quality. This indeed is the quality of the whole modern effort toward a renewal of letters, which ultimately is an expression of an increasing alienation of modern man from the mystery of the Word" (p. 411).

17. *Mystery and Manners*, p. 202.

18. Ibid., pp. 58–59.

19. Ibid., p. 52.

20. Margaret Meaders, "Flannery O'Connor: Literary Witch," *Colorado Quarterly*, 10 (Spring 1962), 384.

21. *Recent Southern Fiction: A Panel Discussion*, Bulletin of Wesleyan College, 41 (January 1961), p. 11.

22. *Mystery and Manners*, p. 207.

23. Ibid., p. 58.

24. Ibid., p. 38.

Notes to Chapter Three

1. *Man's Changing Mask* (Minneapolis: Univ. of Minnesota Press, 1966), p. 92.

2. "The Fiction Writer and His Country," in *The Living Novel: A Symposium*, ed. Granville Hicks (New York: Collier, 1957), p. 164.

3. *Mysticism: A Study in the Nature and Development of Man's Consciousness* (London: Methuen, 1962), passim.

4. Ihab Hassan, *Radical Innocence* (Princeton: Princeton Univ. Press, 1962), p. 79.

5. Joel Wells, "Off the Cuff," *Critic*, 21 (August 1962), 72.

6. Gerard Sherry, "An Interview with Flannery O'Connor," *Critic*, 21 (June 1963), 29.

7. "The Novelist and Free Will," *Fresco*, 1 (Winter 1963), 100.

8. *The Interpreter's Bible*, ed. G. H. Buttrick (New York: Abingdon, 1959), VII, 379.

9. *The Phenomenon of Man* (New York: Harper, 1959), p. 263. The influence of Teilhard de Chardin upon Miss O'Connor's fiction is probably a late development, but one which deserves further scrutiny. Two modest attempts at interpretation can be found in John J. Burke's "Convergence in Flannery O'Connor and Chardin," *Renascence* (Fall 1966), and in George Lensing's "De Chardin's Ideas in Flannery O'Connor," *Renascence* (Summer 1966).

10. *Writer to Writer*, ed. Floyd C. Watkins and Karl F. Knight (New York: Houghton Mifflin, 1966), p. 71.

11. For a much more detailed analysis of the Dantean overtones in this story, see my article, "The City of Woe: Flannery O'Connor's Dantean Vision," *Georgia Review* (Summer 1967).

Notes to Chapter Four

1. "Some Aspects of the Grotesque in Southern Fiction," in *Mystery and Manners*, ed. Sally and Robert Fitzgerald (New York: Farrar, Straus & Giroux, 1969), p. 38.

2. *The Mortal No: Death and the Modern Imagination* (Princeton: Princeton Univ. Press, 1964), p. 292.

3. Alluding to southwestern fiction, Miss O'Connor remarked, "in 19th century American writing there was a great deal of grotesque literature which came from the frontier and was supposed to be funny" (*Mystery and Manners*, pp. 44). The affinities between Miss O'Connor's fiction and this tradition deserve further scrutiny. Willard Thorp has made a preliminary investigation of the subject in "Suggs and Sut in Modern Dress," *Mississippi Quarterly*, 13 (Fall 1960).

4. Readers who wish to see how profoundly Neumann influenced Miss O'Connor in this story should read the former's *The Origins and History of Consciousness* (Princeton: Princeton Univ. Press, 1969) and *The Great Mother* (New York: Pantheon, 1955).

6. "The Human Crisis," *Twice A Year*, Nos. 14–15 (Fall-Winter 1946–47), p. 22. Quoted by Hoffman on p. 269.

7. *Violence in Recent Southern Fiction* (Durham, N.C.: Duke Univ. Press, 1965), p. 78.

8. *Violence: Reflections from a Christian Perspective* (New York: Seabury, 1969), pp. 172–73. I am indebted to Mr. Ellul for his concept of love as a spiritual force and also for his cogent explanation of the incarnation of spiritual forms. The latter, of course, is standard Catholic doctrine. Miss O'Connor, for instance, in referring to Christ rather than the devil, states: "Christ didn't redeem us by a direct intellectual act, but became incarnate in human form, and he speaks to us now through the mediation of a visible Church. All this may seem a long way from the subject of fiction, but it is not, for the main concern of the fiction writer is with mystery as it is incarnated in human life" (*Mystery and Manners*, p. 176).

9. *Mystery and Manners*, pp. 33–34.

10. Ibid., pp. 113–14.

Notes to Chapter Five

1. Katherine Anne Porter, "Gracious Greatness," *Esprit*, 8 (Winter 1964), 56.

2. Joel Wells, "Off the Cuff," *Critic*, 21 (August 1962), 5.

3. "The Role of the Catholic Novelist," *Greyfriar, Siena Studies in Literature*, 7 (Siena College, 1964), 12. This passage is deleted from the version of the essay which the Fitzgeralds reprint in *Mystery and Manners* under the title "Catholic Novelists and Their Readers."

4. "The Fiction Writer and His Country," in *The Living Novel: A Symposium* (New York: Collier, 1957), p. 162.

5. C. Ross Mullins, "Flannery O'Connor: An Interview," *Jubilee*, 11 (June 1963), 33.

6. Ibid., p. 35.

7. "The Church and the Fiction Writer," in *Mystery and Manners*, ed. Sally and Robert Fitzgerald (New York: Farrar, Straus & Giroux, 1969), p. 147. This essay first appeared in *America* (March 30, 1957).

8. "The Novelist and Free Will," *Fresco*, 1 (Winter 1963), 100. Miss O'Connor states that "it is the grandmother's recognition that the Misfit is one of her children" that makes the free acceptance of grace work in

this story. She expands this concept in *Mystery and Manners*: "There is a point in this story where such a gesture [which makes contact with mystery] occurs. The Grandmother is at last alone, facing the Misfit. Her head clears for an instant and she realizes, even in her limited way, that she is responsible for the man before her and joined to him by ties of kinship which have their roots deep in the mystery she has been merely prattling about so far. And at this point, she does the right thing, she makes the right gesture" (pp. 111–12).

9. *Mystery and Manners*, p. 146.

10. "Flannery O'Connor—A Tribute," *Esprit*, 8 (Winter 1964), 37.

11. *Mystery and Manners*, p. 42.

12. Ibid., pp. 148, 151–52.

13. Ibid., pp. 43–44.

14. Ibid., pp. 145–46.

15. Margaret Meaders, "Flannery O'Connor: Literary Witch," *Col orado Quarterly*, 10 (Spring 1962), 384.

16. New York: Farrar, Straus & Giroux, 1961, p. 20. In this essay Miss O'Connor gave her fullest appreciation of Hawthorne, a writer whom she mentioned more than any other in her literary articles, with the exception of Henry James.

Index

Absurd: synonym for grotesque, 6–7
Anderson, Sherwood, 4, 5
"The Artificial Nigger," 28, 54, 55, 56, 60, 71–75, 114

Baptism: in "The River," 59; in *The Violent Bear It Away*, 43,
    62, 64, 65
Barth, John, 4
Baudelaire, Charles, 8, 90
Bernanos, George, 99
Bernard of Clairvaux, Saint, 2
Bierce, Ambrose, 4
Borges, Jorge Luis, 97
Bosch, Hieronymus, 3–4
Breton, André, 12. *See also* surrealism

Camus, Albert, 4, 86
Capote, Truman, 23
Caricature, 10
"The Catholic Novelist in the Protestant South," 39
Child grotesque, 56–67 passim
Christ figure: 17; in "The Displaced Person," 35, 36, 37, 110;
    in "A Good Man Is Hard to Find," 32; in "Parker's Back,"
    37, 38
"The Church and the Fiction Writer," 107
"A Circle in the Fire," 22, 46, 82, 95
Comedy : and the grotesque, 7–8; in names, 10
"The Comforts of Home," 31, 88, 89, 91
Convergence, 70
Cultural grotesque, 38–49 passim

Demonism, 23, 24, 26, 27, 28, 29, 30, 31, 32, 84, 85, 90, 103, 112

Devil, 59, 63, 76, 89, 90, 91, 103, 104, 108
"The Displaced Person," 17, 28, 35, 36, 46, 85, 86, 101, 109, 110, 114
Dostoevsky, Fyodor, 99
Double, psychological, 29, 30, 68

Ellison, Ralph, 36
Ellul, Jacques, 91
"The Enduring Chill," 26, 54, 71, 88, 111
Engle, Paul, 14, 19
Esslin, Martin, 7, 8
"Everything That Rises Must Converge," 54, 69, 70, 88
Exaggeration: use of, 8 10

Faulkner, William, 4, 21, 39, 78, 97, 109
"The Fiction Writer and His Country," 41
Fire: in The Violent Bear It Away, 93–95
Fitzgerald, F. Scott, 5
Free will, 64–65
Frohock, W. M., 85
Fusion. as grotesque technique, 10–11

"The Geranium," 14–16, 53
Gogol, Nikolai, 31
"Good Country People," 10, 11, 22, 27, 78, 79, 91
"A Good Man Is Hard to Find," 9, 11, 22, 31, 32, 53, 77, 78, 79, 81, 93, 98
Gordon, Caroline, 20, 114
Gossett, Louise, 90
Gothicism: in fiction, 4, 12, 107; gothic form, 2, 3; and violence, 77
Grace, 23, 39, 64, 65, 68, 72, 79, 87, 88, 90, 100, 102, 104, 105, 106
"Greenleaf," 46, 82–84, 87, 88

Hawkes, John, 4
Hawthorne, Nathaniel, 27, 54, 74, 109
Hemingway protagonist, 85

Hyman, Stanley Edgar, 63

James, Henry, 51, 105
"Judgment Day," 16, 17, 53

Kafka, Franz, 54
Kayser, Wolfgang, 2, 6, 18, 103

"The Lame Shall Enter First," 8, 9, 22, 26, 56, 60, 87
"A Late Encounter With the Enemy," 9, 26, 41
"The Life You Save May Be Your Own," 10, 32, 33, 34, 78
Lytle, Andrew, 19

Melodrama, 9
Melville, Herman, 35, 109
A Memoir of Mary Ann, 113
Moral and dramatic sense, 51, 54, 55
Myth, 82, 84, 87

Nabokov, Vladimir, 4, 97
Negro: in "The Artificial Nigger," 72–74
Neumann, Eric, 84

O'Connor, William Van, 2

Panofsky, Erwin, 3
"Parker's Back," 17, 37, 38, 43, 95, 96, 104, 111, 114
"The Partridge Festival," 26, 46, 54, 68
Prophecy, 107–109
Purdy, James, 4, 97
Pynchon, Thomas, 4, 97

Quest, 17, 59–75 passim

Radcliffe, Ann, 12
Realism, 11, 22
Regionalism, 38–46 passim
"The Regional Writer," 40

"Revelation," 46–49, 87, 101, 112–113
"The River," 10, 31, 53, 56, 57–60, 104
Romance, 12, 13

Sophocles, 21
Southwestern humor, 4, 80
"A Stroke of Good Fortune," 11, 68
Surrealism, 12, 13

Teilhard de Chardin, 69, 70, 71
"A Temple of the Holy Ghost," 54, 56, 60, 111
Trickster: grotesque, 28, 29, 30, 31, 33; in southwestern humor, 80
Twain, Mark, 33

Underhill, Evelyn, 55

"A View of the Woods," 11, 22, 82
The Violent Bear It Away: exaggeration in, 9, 10; obsession, 24; secular prophets, 25; devil, 31; child grotesque, 60–67; violence, 93, 94, 95, 96, 104

Warren, Robert Penn, 39, 78
Welty, Eudora, 39
West, Nathanael, 4, 20
Williams, Tennessee, 23
Wise Blood: Haze Motes, 17, 23, 24, 25; grotesque trickster, 28, 29, 36, 37; name humor, 10, 68 passim
"Writing Short Stories," 40

Young, Stark, 42